# SURVIVALS
AND
# NEW ARRIVALS

# BOOKS BY HILAIRE BELLOC

*Available From The Publisher*
*In This Series*

Europe and the Faith

William The Conqueror

The Crusades

How the Reformation Happened

Characters of the Reformation

Essays of a Catholic

The Great Heresies

Survivals and New Arrivals

The Crisis of Civilization

# SURVIVALS
### AND
# NEW ARRIVALS

## THE OLD AND NEW ENEMIES
## OF THE CATHOLIC CHURCH

*By*

Hilaire Belloc

TAN BOOKS AND PUBLISHERS, INC.
Rockford, Illinois 61105

Nihil Obstat:      Arthur J. Scanlan
                   Censor Librorum

Imprimatur:    ✠ Patrick Cardinal Hayes
                   Archbishop of New York
                   June 25, 1929

Library of Congress Catalog Card No.:   91-67652

ISBN:   0-89555-454-2

Printed and bound in the United States of America.

TAN BOOKS AND PUBLISHERS, INC.
P.O. Box 424
Rockford, Illinois 61105

1992

To

MY DAUGHTER ELEANOR

# TABLE OF CONTENTS

# 1

## INTRODUCTORY

The curious have remarked that one institution alone for now nineteen hundred years has been attacked not by one opposing principle but from every conceivable point.

It has been denounced upon all sides and for reasons successively incompatible: it has suffered the contempt, the hatred and the ephemeral triumph of enemies as diverse as the diversity of things could produce.

This institution is the Catholic Church.

Alone of moral things present among man it has been rejected, criticized, or cursed, on grounds which have not only varied from age to age, but have been always of conflicting and often of contradictory kinds.

No one attacking force seems to have cared whether its particular form of assault were in agreement with others past, or even contemporary, so long as its assault were directed against Catholicism. Each is so concerned, in each case, with the thing attacked that it ignores all else. Each is indifferent to learn that the very defects it finds in this Institution are elsewhere put forward as the special virtues of some other opponent. Each is at heart concerned not so much with its own doctrine as with the destruction of the Faith.

Thus we have had the Church in Her first days sneered at for insisting on the presence of the full Divine nature in one whom many knew only as a *man;* at the very same time She was called Blasphemous for admitting that a Divine personality could be burdened with a suffering human nature. She was furiously condemned, in later ages, for laxity in discipline and for extravagant severity; for softness in organization and for tyranny; for combating the appetites natural to man, and for allowing them excess and even perversion; for ridiculously putting forward a mass of Jewish folklore as the Word of God, and for neglecting that same Word of God; for reducing everything to reason—that is, to logic, which is the form of reason—and for appealing to mere emotion. Today She is equally condemned for affirming dogmatically the improbable survival of human personality after death, and for refusing to admit necromantic proofs of it—and pronouncing the search for them accursed.

The Church has been presented, and by one set of Her enemies, as based upon the ignorance and folly of Her members—they were either of weak intellect or drawn from the least-instructed classes. By another set of enemies She has been ridiculed as teaching a vainly subtle philosophy, splitting hairs, and so systematizing Her instruction that it needs a trained intelligence to deal with Her theology as a special subject.

This unique experience suffered by the Church, this fact that She alone is attacked from every side, has been appealed to by Her doctors throughout the ages as a proof of Her central position in the scheme of reality; for truth is one and error multiple.

It has also been used as an argument for the unnatural and evil quality of Catholicism that it should have aroused from the first century to the twentieth such varied and unceasing hostility.

But what has been more rarely undertaken, and what is of particular interest to our own day, is an examination of the battle's phases. Which of the attacks are getting old-fashioned? Which new offensives are beginning to appear, and from what direction do they come? Which are the main assaults of the moment? What is the weight of each, and with what success are they being received and thrown back?

I say, this cataloging of the attacks in their order of succession, from these growing outworn in any period to the new ones just appearing, has been neglected. A general view of the procession is rarely taken. Yet to make such an appreciation should be of value. The situation of the Church at any one time can be estimated only by noting what forms of attack are failing, and why;

with what degree of resistance the still vigorous ones are being combated; what novel forms of offensive are appearing. It is only so that we can judge how the whole position stood or stands in any one historical period.

Now the historical period in which we have most practical interest is our own. To grasp the situation of the Catholic Church *today* we must appreciate which of the forces opposing her are *today* growing feeble, which are *today* in full vigor, which are *today* appearing as new antagonists, hardly yet in their vigor but increasing.

As for the Faith itself it stands immovable in the midst of all such hostile things; they arise and pass before that majestic presence:

*Stat et stabit, manet et manebit: spectator orbis.*

Let us note at the outset that the result of our examination (the true position of the Catholic Church today, and Her chances of triumph or defeat) is of the most urgent and immediate importance to all our civilization. There is no other judgment concerning the fate of mankind—and particularly of our own European civilization with its extensions in the New World—compatible in significance to a just estimate of the strength and chances of the Catholic Church. There is no other matter on the same level of interest. That interest is of the same absorbing kind to the man who regards the Faith as an illusion, to the man who hates it as an enemy, and to the man who accepts it as the only authoritative voice on earth.

How Catholicism stands today is obviously a vital matter both to the man who recognizes it for the salvation of the world, and to the man who regards it as a mortal poison in society. But it is also a vital matter to any neutral observer who has enough history to know that *religion* is at the root of every culture, and that on the rise and fall of *religions* the great changes of society have depended.

Were human society molded by material environment the fate of no spiritual institution, however august or widespread, would be of final moment. A new mechanical invention, a new turn in the external mode of life, would be the thing to note and the thing upon which we might base our judgment of human fates.

But it is not so. The form of any society ultimately depends upon its philosophy, upon its way of looking at the universe, upon its judgment of moral values: that is, in the concrete, upon its religion.

For whether it calls its philosophy by the name of "religion" or no, into what *is,* in practice, a religion of some kind, the philosophy of any society ultimately falls. The ultimate source of social form is the attitude of the mind; and at the heart of every culture is a creed and code of morals: expressed or taken for granted.

If it were true that economic circumstances mainly decided the fate of society (and that is a more respectable error than the mechanical, for every human economic system or discovery or adaptation, proceeds from the mind) then we might waste our time, as so many do today, on discussing economic tendencies as determining the future of man. But it is not true that economic circumstance molds our destiny. Industrial Capitalism, for instance, did not develop of itself: it was the slow product of false religion. It arose out of the Reformation; and in particular from the influence of Calvin. But for the Reformation that economic arrangement would not be troubling us today. Its root is still in religion; a change in religion would kill it and its attendant parasite called Socialism.

Again, chattel slavery in the West slowly disappeared under the influence of the Catholic Church. There are those who regret its disappearance; the majority of us have been taught to approve its disappearance: at any rate it disappeared.

A group of intellectuals have argued that the gradual action of a Catholicism had no such effect upon the pagan world, and that the slow dissolution of slavery (it took more than a thousand years) was a function of material environment. They are wrong. The old, absolute, pagan slavery which seemed essential to civilized society slowly dissolved because it was incompatible with the Catholic doctrine. It was not directly condemned by the Church, but it proved indirectly unable to live in an atmosphere not pagan. It had to be modified; and once it began to be modified it had started on its long road to dissolution: the slave became a serf, the serf a peasant. And by just so much as society is sinking back into paganism today, by just so much the institution of slavery begins to reappear in the new laws regulating labor.

Neither brute material circumstance, though it is of great effect on society, nor more subtle economic arrangement is the ultimate framer of human politics. As we proceed deeply and more deeply from cause to cause we discover that what gives its nature to a human group is its attitude towards The Last Things: its conception of the End of Man.

Even when a positive creed has lost its vigor and dwindled under indifference, its remaining effect upon the stuff of society remains profound.

Should any doubt this let them mark the effects of the two contrasted religious cultures in the West: the Protestant and Catholic; that proceeding from the schism in the sixteenth century, and that which, in the sixteenth century, weathered the storm and maintained tradition.

All may see the ease with which industrialism grows in a soil of Protestant culture, the difficulty with which it grows in a soil of ancient Catholic culture.

In the latter, whether that difficulty take the form of negligence or of revolt, it is equally apparent. Industrialism has flourished under Prussia, as in England and the United States; it has starved in Ireland and Spain; it menaces civil war in France and Italy. It is indeed a common matter of reproach against the Catholic culture that there has been such friction between it and the industrial system. (It is true that hypocrisy hesitates to use the words "Catholic Culture." But when it talks of "Celt" or "Latin," Catholicism is what hypocrisy means by such terms.)

Again, if we look at the grouping of national policies today in Europe, we at once discover the effect of a common religious sympathy. Why else do we hear sneers against the Pole, the Italian, the Frenchman, the Spaniard, the Belgian, and a corresponding admiration for the Dutch, the Scandinavians, the Prussians?

His popular press and fiction hide from the townsman of today this elementary truth, that upon religion all turns, and that every main political problem, every main economic one, is finally a function of the philosophy which is at work beneath all. He hears of "race" as the ultimate factor. He even hears of "Nordic," "Alpine," "Mediterranean." His attention is drawn to physical conditions: the presence of coal or of ports. Meanwhile the major cause of all social difference is left unmentioned.

It would be interesting, had I the space, to consider the causes of this strange silence. It is most profound in England though there the most glaring examples of religious effect are beneath the eyes of all: Scotland for centuries the fierce enemy of England now fallen into one commonwealth with her through a common ethical system; Ireland increasingly hostile and now at last separated.

There is another cause, the truth which all should feel in appreciating the present situation of Catholicism. It is the fact that the Church is unique. The line of cleavage throughout the world lies between what is with, and what is against, the Faith.

If it were true that the modern world is full of warring creeds, then the situation of the Catholic Church would not be of that transcendent interest. She could not claim to be one of many moral institutions, each based on separate doctrines: Her creed one of many creeds; and we might debate with solemn stupidity (as indeed our contemporaries do debate) whether this, that, or the other, among many sects and opinions, were of the greater value or had the greater chance of survival.

But that is not the situation at all. There is no parallel between the Catholic Church and any other institution. There is no parallel between the Catholic Church and any other man-made grouping of opinions or of moods. She is wholly distinct. As with Her Founder, so with Her: all that is not of Her is against Her; for She claims, and Her adherents maintain the claim, that Hers is the one and the only authoritative voice upon earth.

Her doctrines are not conclusions arrived at by experiment, nor slipped into by personal emotion. Still less are they opinions, probabilities, fashions. Her corporate unity is not one of which others are tolerant, or which is itself tolerant of others. She has no borderland of partial agreement with error nor is there a flux or common meeting place between Herself and things more or less similar, more or less neighborly. She has frontiers rigidly defined: not only in Her doctrine and its claim to divinity but in Her very stuff and savor. Within Her walls all is of one kind; without, all is of another.

It is abundantly clear to those who are members of this Institution that it thus presents throughout the world a unique personality. It is becoming clear to most who are not members. The Church is loved and hated in a degree greater than that which measures other loves or hatreds: even those between nations in our modern fever of exalted nationalism. The loyalty She obtains is more vivid than that produced even by modern patriotism. The hatred She arouses is stronger than the hatred felt for an enemy in arms. And these loves and hatreds have immediate and tremendous reactions upon all around.

Take one example of Her unique character. The Catholic Church is the one bulwark today against the probably ephemeral but still very dangerous conflagration called Communism. Take another and more profound example: She is the one stronghold against modern pantheism, and its accompanying chaos in art and morals.

There is, then, no man who cares to understand the character of the world but must acquaint himself with the situation of the Faith. What are its present enemies? What dangers beset it? Where and how is it checked? Where lies its opportunities for growth? These are the outstanding questions. Compared with a judgment upon the present situation of the Catholic Church, a judgment upon the rise and fall of economic systems or of nations is insignificant.

This is my postulate, and the outset of my inquiry.

\* \* \*

I have said that the situation of the Church at any moment (and therefore in our own time) is best appreciated by judging the rise and decline of the forces opposing Her at that moment.

Now these, when we pause to estimate the state of the battle in any one phase of it, fall into three fairly distinct groups:

*(i)* There is, most prominent, what I will call the *Main Opposition* of the moment. Thus in the fourth and fifth centuries Arianism filled the sky. The Faith seemed in peril of death no longer from official and heathen persecution but from internal disruption. The new Heresy supported by the Roman armies and their generals, not only in the east but in Gaul, in Italy, Africa and Spain, seemed an attack too strong for the Church to survive. Society was military then, and the soldiers were Arian. In the seventh and eighth centuries the Arian attack first rapidly declines then wholly passes; the Mahommedan rises gigantic against us. In the ninth and tenth, to the Mahommedans are added the Heathen pirates of the north, and the eastern Mongol hordes. In the eleventh and twelfth the danger lies in a rationalizing movement *from within,* against the Sacramental mysteries and later against the Hierarchy.

*(ii)* At any moment there lie upon one side of the Main opposition old forms of attack which are gradually leaving the field—I will call them The *Survivals.*

*(iii)* There are, on the other side, new forms of attack barely entering the field. These I will call The *New Arrivals.*

The Survivals exemplify the endless, but always perilous, triumph of the Faith by their defeat and gradual abandonment of the struggle. A just appreciation of them makes one understand where the weakness of the main attack, which they preceded and in part caused, may lie. The New Arrivals exemplify the truth that the Church will never be at peace, and a just appreciation of them enables us to forecast in some degree the difficulties of tomorrow.

Between the two, Survivals and New Arrivals, we can more fully gauge the character of the Main Action and only in a survey of all three can we see how the whole situation lies. For such reasons is a survey of the kind essential to a full comprehension of the age.

We have lost much by the paucity of such testimony in the past, due perhaps to the fact that in the heat of battle men cannot be troubled with the general surveys.

Men tell us amply how the Main Action of their time raged. We hear all about Jansenism and Puritanism in the seventeenth century, and all about nationalism immediately after; but very briefly and disconnectedly do we hear what were the *last* efforts of older enemies in each period, and still more scrappily, or not at all, do they tell us of approaching *new* ones. Indeed, these last are only to be guessed at, as a rule, from indications which contemporaries misunderstood: because the beginnings of a new form of attack are small, scattered and hidden. It is not usually until the offensive has developed that men are awake to it.

In the records of the Past, then, descriptions of the gradual decline of old forms of attack and the indications of new ones arriving are imperfect or absent.

Yet how interesting would it be if we had (for instance) some such view of the end of the seventeenth century, in which the author should describe the effect upon his time of the failing Puritanical and Jansenist movement, and the advent of the rationalist, which was just beginning to show the tips of its ears! How interesting it would be to have someone presenting in the eleventh or early twelfth century the decline of the brute, external, pagan and Mahommedan attack in arms and the appearance of the new, more subtle, philosophic poison from within!

In the following pages I propose to attempt something of the kind for the time in which we live: hence have I used this title "Survivals and New Arrivals." I do not pretend to a detailed study: I am writing no more than a general survey, the interest of which, to its author at any rate, lies both on the intellectual and on the comic side. For there enters an element of *Comedy* (in the full sense of that great word) whenever we watch the death or passing of a human mood which had thought itself absolute and eternal. There is a high comedy in discovering new moods still timid or struggling, which will in their turn affirm themselves to be indestructible, and in their turn will die. To this comic interest is added another of a very practical kind: forewarned is forearmed.

Thus, to make two particular examples out of several with which I shall deal: The old Bible Christian offensive is a

Survival pretty well done for. No one will deny the comic side of its exhaustion. The recognition of that comedy is no bar to sympathy with its pathetic side. There is something very gallant about these Literalists. They never retreated, they never surrendered, they were incapable of maneuver, and the few that remain will die where they stand rather than give way a foot. Their simplicity sometimes has a holy quality about it. On the other hand, of the New Arrivals, you see, among the forces beginning to organize themselves against the Faith, a denial of human responsibility and even of personality: a denial that would have seemed fantastic and insane in the eyes of all those attacking the Church, from no matter what angle, only a generation ago. And that is comic too: when Professor Schmidt says: "I cannot help doing all I do. I have no will. And what is more, there is no Professor Schmidt."

I must make a further apology before I begin my consideration of these Survivals and New Arrivals, which is, that my sketches will necessarily suffer from a defect of locality. I am naturally better acquainted with Survivals and New Arrivals in the society I inhabit, than I am with those of foreign countries, and though the problem is universal as the Church is, I must deal with men and writings, particular opinions, which have hardly been heard of by those who are not acquainted with the English tongue.

No one, for instance, is in French eyes a more perfect example of a Survival than Paul Souday or more widely known; yet in England his name is not heard. Or again, certain of the new fancy religions, such as Christian Science, have real weight with us; while a Frenchman would use of them the word *"fumisterie"* or even *"blague."* He would not take them seriously for a moment. What is more, he would imagine that their adherents did not take them seriously: in which he would be wrong.

Such, then, are the limits and necessary defects of the task upon which I shall now set out. I shall accomplish it most imperfectly, but I hope to leave a general impression the outline of which shall be true.

# 2

## THE TWO CULTURES

Before we can understand the relative importance of the forces moving against the Catholic Church today, we must grasp the fact that She exists, in our divided and chaotic civilization, among three widely different surroundings. The way in which each of these affects the life of the Faith modifies, locally, every problem connected with Catholicism. In one, a particular Survival will be of high importance, which, in another, will be of little or none. In one a New Arrival appearing against Catholicism is already formidable, while in another it is unknown.

For if we look around us at the present situation of the Catholic Church in the modern world of Europe, and in the expansion of Europeans into Asia and the New World, we find Her living in three media or atmospheres, each hostile to Her, but each hostile in a very different manner from the others.

In all these three provinces the Catholic Church has long lost, and nowhere in any part of them regained, Her old and native position as the exclusive and established religion of society, with full official status, and the support of the civil power for Her authority. But Her own attitude towards the alien dominating civil authority, its attitude towards Her, varies in very nature from one to the other. Still more do the social atmospheres of each and Her own reactions in those atmospheres differ from one to the other.

These three provinces, with their three very distinct attitudes towards the Faith, are:

(1) The culture attached, historically at least, to the Greek Church;

(2) the Protestant culture; and

(3) the old Catholic culture.

I omit in this connection the situation of the Catholic Church *as it is now* in Mahommedan and pagan countries, for there it still normally follows the condition either of the European (or American) countries whence its missionaries proceed or of the European (or American) country ruling the particular district of paganism or Mahommedanism concerned.

In the Greek culture (including, of course, what is its chief part, the vast area at present controlled by the Soviet Government) the situation of the Church is, so far, that of an imperceptible minority. There are exceptions in particular provinces—for instance, where the Italians control an Aegean Island—but take the enormous area as a whole (with a total population not much less than 200 millions) the numerical proportion of Catholics therein is negligible, their social importance equally negligible.

The same cannot be said of their spiritual effect; the effect, that is, provoked by Catholic thought, occasionally, upon intellectual groups of some importance in leadership. But, generally speaking, the tiny fragment of Catholicism is drowned in that vast sea of the Orthodox culture. There is talk, indeed, and hope of some great Catholic development acting through the spiritual void left by the recent revolution in Russia; but that is for the future.

We must nonetheless remark that the Soviet revolution has shaken all the world of Greek culture to its foundations. Before it took place the whole of that culture ultimately depended, directly or indirectly, upon the armed might of the Russian Autocracy. The Czardom was the nucleus or foundation of all the Greek-Church culture; it was the essential institution; it was the central post on which all the fabric leaned. It made of the Orthodox religion a powerful monopoly; it acted positively and urgently for the forcible exclusion of Catholicism, not only in Russia but, for instance, in Serbia, where the example was copied. All that has gone to pieces.

The Soviet Government in spite of certain recent changes remains predominantly Jewish, not only in the personnel of its secret police within and of its propagandists without, but in its moral character and methods. Not perhaps because it is Jewish, but certainly because it is Bolshevist, it has as strong a hatred for the Greek Church as for Catholicism; perhaps in a final issue it would make its chief object of attack throughout the world that which it felt to be the most living force; and this is, without question, the Catholic Church. But the general position, so far as the Catholic Church in Greek countries (and particularly in Russia) is concerned, is so far little changed by the huge upheaval, She remains almost unknown to the mass of the people.

There is indeed one recent exception to be remembered. This exception is the precarious subjection of the Catholic Croats and Slovenes to the orthodox power of Serbia. The incompetent politicians who imposed their own confusion of mind and their own ignorance of history upon Christendom after the Great War, tied, not federally, but absolutely, a considerable body of Catholic culture to a dynasty, a capital and a government not its own: the dynasty and government of Belgrade. A large Catholic district was artificially sewn on, as it were, to the edges of the Orthodox peoples. Thus, politically, a new kingdom called Jugo-Slavia has, to its original Orthodox half, another half, as large, attached; and this new piece is Catholic in culture and western in script and all the details of life. We have already seen the disastrous consequences of that blunder.

Similarly Roumania has had attached to it a body roughly doubling its size, most of the inhabitants of which are either Latin Catholics or Uniate Catholics.

These anomalies, which have arisen from the crudity of our Parliamentarians, somewhat obscure the issue. But it remains true that in the area of the Orthodox or Greek Church culture the situation of Catholicism is one of such slight influence that we may for the moment neglect it. The real issue is between the situation of Catholicism in the area of Protestant culture and in the area of the old Catholic culture; and between the state of the Church in the one and Her state in the other lies a contrast such as the past history of our race never knew.

The area of the Protestant culture is formed by the United States of America, Canada as a whole (with the exception of the solid French-Canadian corner), Great Britain, Australasia and the Cape, Holland, North Germany, Scandinavia, and the Baltic States, excepting Lithuania.

In this area there are two things to be remarked. First that the degree in which the Catholic Church is known in the various parts of this culture, through its numerical proportion or moral influence, varies greatly; next, that this area of culture contains one province of a peculiar kind upon which one must speak specially if one is to avoid an erroneous conclusion—that province is the Prusso-German Empire, or Reich.

The Scandinavian countries, which are almost entirely Protestant, are small, and do not largely affect the general situation today. Another of the lesser countries, Holland, has a very large, active and well-organized Catholic minority, a great deal more than a third of the nation—indeed, nearer 5/12ths—but the traditions, political and social, of Holland are opposed to Catholicism, for Holland arose as an independent nation by a financial revolt against its monarch, Philip II, who stood in his time for the Church against the Reformation; and all the energies of its governing class were, for two hundred years, directed against Catholicism.

But in that Prussian system which is best named today "The Reich," and which has come to be popularly, though erroneously, called "Germany," a special condition of affairs was established by the genius of Bismarck.

Bismarck determined to divert the strong desire for German unity to the advantage of his own kingdom of Prussia and its ruling dynasty, the Hohenzollerns, whom he served. He therefore created a so-called "German Empire," which was to be the very negation of what the old words "German" and "Imperial" had meant for a thousand years. He deliberately designed it to contain the largest possible minority of Catholics consistent with leaving the majority of the new State Protestant and under the direct and indirect control of Berlin. Had he worked for a union of all German-speaking peoples he would have included Austria and the German parts of Bohemia, and he would have formed a State where the two cultures would have balanced each other. The word "German" would not connote for us—as it now does—the idea of "Anti-Catholic," nor would one of the principal Catholic bodies in the world—the Germans of the Rhine and Danube—have fallen asunder and, in losing their unity, lost their power.

As it is, we have the State which Bismarck artificially framed still existing among us, strongly organized, and in the peculiar situation of being directed from the Protestant culture, leaving the Catholic culture within it active and free yet politically dominated by an anti-Catholic tradition and standing before the world as part of the Protestant culture.

If one were to call the German Reich, as a whole, Protestant, there would be natural and justified protest from those portions of it in the south and west which are not only Catholic and strongly so, but for the most part Catholic in homogeneous bodies, with memories of comparatively recent local sovereignty, some fragments of which remain. Indeed the Catholics of the Reich amount to just a third of its whole population.

On the other hand, if one were to say of this Catholic element in the Reich that it was a separate affair, belonging to the Catholic culture as a whole, one would be still more wrong. The Catholic portions of the Reich are not forcibly joined to a greater anti-Catholic portion as are the newly annexed parts of Jugo-Slavia or Roumania, but they are still bound into the new state created by Bismarck for the benefit of Prussia.

Common great victories won sixty years ago, very strong common influences, accompanied by a great expansion in wealth and in population and a very striking development in all forms of civic activity, the founding of a whole new social system, a well-maintained internal order—all these things have welded Bismarck's Reich together. We thus have, as regards the situation of the Faith here, this anomaly; that, though very far from homogeneous in religion, *as a unit* the Reich counts in the eyes of foreigners as part of the Protestant culture. It attracts the sympathy of Protestant nations such as England and Scandinavia; its own hostility is rather directed against neighboring Catholic Powers such as Poland and France.

The Reich, then, not only contains a large minority of Catholics, but of Catholics particularly devoted to their religion, but this Catholic minority of the Reich, though culturally similar to a considerable German Catholic body beyond the nominal frontier (the main part of them are in Catholic Austria), is politically separate from its fellows. Should the future see a union of Austria with the Reich the whole character of Central Europe would be transformed and the work of Bismarck destroyed.

Such is the situation of Catholicism in those states of Continental Europe which have a Protestant tradition and direction.

When we turn to the particular case of the English-speaking world (outside Ireland) we find a situation quite different from that of the rest of the Protestant culture, because its history has been different. In almost all other aspects the term "English-speaking world" is a misnomer. The "English-speaking world" represents no reality to which can be properly attached one name. But in this one (and capital) matter of Catholicism the term is exact. With the exception of Ireland the area covered by English speech—that is, Great Britain, the white Dominions, and the United States—have a character of their own so far as the Catholic Church is concerned.

The English-speaking world, though now morally broken up, had a common root. Its institutions, at their origin, sprang from the English Protestant seventeenth century.

The American social groups arose for the most part as emigrant colonies with a definitely religious origin, and nearly all of them with an origin strongly anti-Catholic. In England, Scotland and Wales the Catholic Church had been defeated by 1605. Even at the highest estimate and including all who vaguely sympathized with Catholicism, we find it was by 1688 no more than a seventh or an eighth of England in numbers, much less of Scotland, and in both countries failing. It dwindled after 1688 to a tiny fragment—about one percent—and that pitiful atom was of no account in the national life nor of any effect on national institutions. From such a source flowed first the colonial system of America, next that of the Dominions. Of course, so general a statement needs modification. South Africa was, and may again be, Dutch; the New World had Dutch origins in one of its states and Catholic traditions in two others. But, in outline, the generalization is true.

The stuff of all this culture was one from which Catholicism had been driven out, and till the mid-nineteenth century the United States, Great Britain and her Colonies had little need to reckon with the Faith within their own boundaries.

In our own time all that has largely changed. The chief agent of the change has been the Irish people dispersed by the famine. They brought a large Catholic body into England, Australasia, Canada and America. There has also been more recently a large immigration into the United States from other districts of Catholic culture—Poles, South Germans, Italians.

There has been to some extent in the United States, but probably with much more effect in Britain, a movement of conversion. This movement has not largely affected numbers, but it has had a profound moral effect, because it has touched so many leaders of thought, so many general writers, and latterly, even, so many historians.

For example, the Catholic bodies in the two ancient universities of England number, I suppose, hardly one-fifteenth, perhaps not more than one-twentieth, of the whole. In the teaching body they are hardly present, and such very few as are may not spread the Faith. But no one can say that Oxford and Cambridge are not aware of Catholicism today.

For these various causes Catholic minorities and Catholic influences have appeared in the English-speaking world, but have appeared in societies of an historical foundation different from that upon which other parts of the Protestant culture repose.

In these you have either the conditions of Scandinavia and the Baltic Protestants—with no appreciable Catholicism present—or the conditions of the German Reich and Holland where a very large Catholic population is part of the State, where the boundaries of the State have been traced with the very object of including the largest Catholic minority compatible with Protestant domination, where the character of Catholicism is familiar to all, holding an ancient historic position, and where large Catholic societies of the same blood and speech lie just over the frontiers. Catholic literature, ideas, history are known. But in the English-speaking world it is otherwise. *There* Catholicism reentered late as an alien phenomenon after the character of society had become "set" in an anti-Catholic mold. There all national literature, traditions, law and especially history were (and are) fundamentally anti-Catholic. All the Philosophy of Society was long settled in the anti-Catholic mood before the first recrudescence of Catholicism appeared.

Therefore it is inevitable that the Catholic body within this English-speaking world should breathe an air which is not its own and should be more affected by a non-Catholic or anti-Catholic spirit than could be possible in the other Protestant nations wherein an ancient Catholic culture exists with unbroken traditions.

There has thus been produced in Britain and the United States a situation the like of which has not existed before in the whole history of the Catholic Church since Constantine. It is a situation of very powerful effect upon the general fortunes of our race today throughout the world, because the English-speaking communities are for the moment so wealthy and numerous.

It leads, among other things, to an atmosphere of debate rather than of combat, which every general observer must have noticed. It also leads to the conception of proportional claim; that is, the claim of the Catholic minority, even when it is small, not to be forbidden (by *direct* means) access to positions and public advantages in the general body. Conversely it leads (as in the case of University teaching just mentioned) to the use of *indirect* means for the prevention of Catholic progress.

It is a position rapidly developing; it is one the future of which cannot, of course, be determined—on that account it is the more interesting. But it is one which certainly will change. That is almost the only thing one can predicate about it. What began as a persecuted thing and went on as a tolerated anomaly has turned into a regular constituent of the State, but a constituent differing in quality from the rest of the State.

One effect is the close interaction between such Catholic minorities and the non-Catholic English-speaking world around them. One man will call it absorption of the Catholic body into the non-Catholic air which is about it upon every side; another would call it the very opposite—would say that into that non-Catholic air was infiltrating a measure of Catholic ideas. The fact that these two contradictory views are so widely held proves that mutual reaction is strong.

Another effect is the comparative lack of sympathy, politically at least, between these Catholic minorities and the great bodies of Catholic culture abroad.

The political quarrels of these great foreign bodies are either ill-understood or ignored in the English-speaking world, or, at the best, even in the case of widely travelled men with a large Continental connection, rouse no great interest (let alone enthusiasm!) in the Catholics of England and the United States.

You may say, for instance, that the Catholic body in England is slightly less hostile to the Polish cause than the run of Englishmen are, but you cannot say that they know much about Poland, or that one in a hundred of them has any marked sympathy with Polish resistance to Prussia. Similarly the great body of literature in the Catholic culture is closed to these minorities of Catholics in the English-speaking world. They have no powerful daily press. They get nearly all their news and more than half their ideas from papers anti-Catholic in direction. The books which make the mind of the nation help to make the mind of its Catholic minority—and that literature is, in bulk, vividly anti-Catholic.

My own experience of this lies especially in the department of history. The whole story of Europe looks quite different when you see it from the point of view of the average cultivated Frenchman or Italian from what it does in the eyes of the average educated English or American Catholic.

So much is this the case that the statement of what is a commonplace upon the Continent appears as a paradox to most

Catholics in England.

The past, especially the remote past, is another world to them. All the belauding of the break-up of Christendom in the sixteenth century, all the taking for granted of its political consequence as a good thing, all denunciation of our champions, all the flattery of our worst enemies, all the sneers at nations which kept the Faith, all admiration of the Princes and Politicians who destroyed it are absorbed by us in the books on which we are bred. A ridicule and hatred of the later Stuarts at home, of Louis XIV abroad: a respect at least for the House of Orange: an insistence on the decline of Spain: all this and the whole mass of English letters train us in special pleading against the Faith. Nor have we, in England at least, any bulk of true history (as yet) to counteract this flood of propaganda.

But before closing these remarks upon the position of Catholics in the English-speaking Protestant countries, one point must be observed in modification: the Catholic, even under such favorable surroundings, has the advantage over his opponents both in definition and in knowledge. He knows much more about the others than the others know about him.

Further the Catholic has a philosophy which applies to all the practice of life and which does not change, while in the world about him there is neither a united philosophy nor even fixity in the moods of the time. This contrast is increasingly noticeable as the dogmas of Protestantism and its social rules dissolve.

The Catholic Church has, then, in that English-speaking world with which the readers (and writer) of this book are principally concerned, such advantages and disadvantages. It is badly cut off from the general Catholic world outside. It is permeated by an anti-Catholic literature, social custom and history. On the other hand it reacts upon that hostile atmosphere and perceives, though dimly, some of its inherent superiorities: notably in clarity of thought and a determined philosophy.

The disabilities of the Faith in such an air are closely connected with that modern cross-religion of Nationalism of which I shall speak in more detail when I come to the main modern opponents of the Church.

The mark of the Catholic situation in all this area of Protestant culture is toleration *upon a basis of Nationalism.*

Worship the Nation and you may hold what lesser opinions you please. Whether the Catholic body be very small and poor, as in Great Britain, or a strong locally grouped and politically influential, mainly urban, minority as in America (the estimates of this differ—some, I believe, would call it a sixth of the population); whether it be very large indeed as in Australia and Canada, or smaller as in New Zealand, everywhere this mark is apparent.

Therefore the Faith is treated as one among many sects within one nation: and we tend to accept that position. The modern Protestant doctrine, that sects, that is, opinions, have a sacred right to existence "so long as they obey the law," the idea that the State has a right of legislation against which no moral appeal can lie—let alone the legislative power of the Church; the inability of those who think thus to see that toleration and conformity with every law make a contradiction of terms: all these create the social atmosphere in which we live. The particular practice of Catholicism may be continued without hindrance; we may hear Mass. Certain characteristic products of Catholicism may develop unimpeded. For instance, the religious orders enjoy complete freedom in every part of this world, they possess property without limit, and spread and build without restriction. But all is within and beneath civil society.

Again, what is most important, the Catholic educational system is safeguarded in the English-speaking Protestant world. It is safeguarded in different ways and in different degrees in different places. Thus in England it enjoys public revenue. In the United States it does not enjoy that revenue, but it is allowed every opportunity for voluntary extension. But all is under the supreme worship of Caesar.

The truth I here emphasize is unpalatable. Most of us are only half aware (and are becoming less aware with every added decade), that the air we breathe is anti-Catholic; that the history we are taught, the moral ideas behind the legal system we obey, the restrictions imposed on us, the political conceptions embodied in every public act, the general attitude toward foreign countries, are all the products of that Nationalism which their non-Catholic fellow-citizens regard as *the* sacred emotion. We cannot but be ourselves filled with that emotion. But it is spiritually at issue with the Faith.

\* \* \*

So far I have dealt mainly, as being our chief concern, with the situation of the Catholic Church in the English-speaking world as a preparation for judging its reception of both decaying and growing antagonisms.

To appreciate the effect of these as a whole, let us glance at the situation in the countries of ancient Catholic culture, such as France, Spain and Italy, where there reign conditions very different from our own; for that purpose, let us consider the origins; since we shall not fully understand this important dual character attaching to the present political position of the Catholic Church in the world unless we appreciate how it came about through the past.

The great battle of the Reformation ended without victory for either side, legitimate or rebel. The opposing armies arrived at no decision, but retired from the field and divided Europe between them. Nearly three hundred years ago, at the Peace of Westphalia, the main struggle was concluded; even the last act in the tragedy, the English Revolution, is now already nearly two and a half centuries old.

The nations which came out of that conflict with their national traditions saved, and the Church still giving the tone of society, kept all their principal institutions closely bound up with the Catholic Church—notably, of course, their national dynasties; and those national dynasties were for the most part absolute monarchies: that is, Governments in which the whole nation was ruled from one center, supporting the weak against the strong and curbing the influence of riches.

Further, in these nations, the general order of society was based upon the same hierarchic conception as is to be found in the hieratic organization of the Catholic Church. Power came in regular descent, and there was an exact order.

It must further be remembered that all the principal acts of the State were interwoven closely with the official life of the Church.

The union was a much more real and living a thing than the connection to be found between governments and established churches elsewhere.

The bishops were great political figures and of real weight in administration; the king was crowned and anointed in a function essentially Catholic, and dating back for far more than a thousand years; the administration of justice was everywhere in touch with the Catholic doctrine and opinion. The Crucifix stood in the Courts, the morals and social ideas of Catholicism governed their procedure.

Moreover, these Catholic States imposed the official religion, and had the great majority of the people at their back in so imposing it. In the various Italian States, in the Spanish Netherlands (which today we call Belgium), in France and Spain, the principal appointments went only to those of the national religion. The educational system of the country was as deeply impregnated with the same spirit.

It is difficult for a man living under modern English or American conditions to visualize such a state of affairs. Even if modern England were what it most certainly is not, co-extensive with the Established Church of England, and if that Church had a large body of definite doctrine and a mass of uniformed detailed observance as well, then there would be some parallel. In modern conditions in America one can discover no parallel at all.

Well, this state of affairs came to an end actually in France, potentially in other Catholic countries, by the action of the French Revolution.

Long before the French Revolution a wide intellectual movement of skepticism, which was actively hostile to the Church, had run through all Catholic society, particularly in France, but the official structure remained the same until the Revolution.

After the Revolution that structure crashed. There was torn a rent in the hitherto inextricable close web of the Church and political society. The theory was promulgated and acted upon that civil society alone could hold legitimate power and that the Faith was no more than the opinion of individual citizens who, even if they were very numerous, even if they were the bulk of the nation, had no right to make their private religion the note of institutions which concerned all men, non-Catholic as well as Catholic.

Thus a definite quarrel was set between the old official position of the Church, including its old wealth and its old political power, on the one side, and on the other a theory that the Church was not the business of the State and no more than a set of people who happened to use devotions which did not concern the Government or the institutions of the nation.

Now the essential point to seize in the nations of Ancient Catholic Culture, the nations which withstood the storm of the Reformation and maintained their traditions intact, is that this quarrel has never yet been decided. The old security and unquestioned position of the official church which remained standing for five lifetimes after the Reformation while all its moral invisible supports were silently crumbling, was never the same after 1791. The French Revolutionary armies carried on the new lay conception of the State into Belgium, into Spain, into Italy, into Catholic Germany. Literature and teaching continued their effect. The *idea* of the Lay State (though nowhere perfectly realized and everywhere combated) overspread all Catholic Europe.

But neither the official Church nor the Catholic conscience ever admitted this lay theory of the State. The Church continued to claim her political place as part of her theory of Catholic society; and all Catholics—in every case the bulk of the nations concerned—felt that it was Her *right*.

To take a test instance, the Church claimed a special position in education. She called it essential to society that the elementary schools should teach Catholic doctrine to the children and the Catholic philosophy should permeate the universities. The lay conception of the State fought, and continues to fight, this claim as a tyranny and an anomaly.

And the main thing to grasp, if we are to understand this

mighty political problem of "Laicism" (which is so little known outside the nations of the Catholic culture), is the fact already emphasized: that the struggle is still proceeding. The conception of the laical state which looked like winning hands down fifty years ago has not even achieved an uncertain victory; the Catholic ideal, though more sympathetic to the new strong and healthy movements in Italy and Spain, is not supreme in those states over the Laic. The two parties are still standing on their positions.

The laical ideal in education still appeals to the logic of the man who thinks of religion as a private opinion, and usually as an illusion at that. But to the average parent in a Catholic country, the so-called neutrality of the lay school and university is still felt to be a sham. Its neutrality is not in his eyes a real neutrality, it is a form of persecution and, still more, a policy designed to uproot the Faith.

There is no reconciliation between the two positions, because they start from different first principles, which run through every function of civic life; not only education, but administration, justice and everything else.

The Catholic Position starts with the first principle that a homogeneous Catholic society with Church and State closely bound up together is the ideal; and that ideal, remember, is not something vague to be aimed at in the future, it is a living historical memory of recent date, even in some districts a thing experienced within living memory and to others half restored.

For instance, it is only half a lifetime ago that the Crucifix was taken away from the Courts of Justice in France; and in Italy, as we know, it has recently been put back. In Spain, after more than one interlude of the laical state, the union of Church and State has been established. In Poland the proposal to make Catholicism the established State Religion was defeated only with difficulty. It will be renewed.

Take, then, the Catholic culture as a whole, and you see present in it a political situation not comparable to that in England or America. You see a political situation of conflict not yet decided, with a strict, wide, strongly historical claim on the

Catholic side to establishment and State recognition; a claim, expectant only in some countries, partly realized in others, but everywhere vigorously alive.

This brief introductory sketch of the Catholic position in Catholic societies it was necessary to add to that of the Church in the Protestant culture before approaching an analysis of the older and newer forces arrayed against the Faith today, because those forces differ in character according to the culture in which they act.

To them will I now proceed, and I will open with the SURVIVALS, beginning with the more venerable of the group, those which are *in articulo mortis* and yielding up the ghost before our eyes, and going on in order through the less moribund to the most active.

# 3

## SURVIVALS

I propose in this section to take the main Survivals of old forms of attack upon the Catholic Church. I mean by these, forms of attack which, though no longer in the first rank, are present amongst us, if not all of them in all parts of the modern world at any rate each in some contemporary part. I shall not include those which are fairly dead and buried (say, Voltaire's *Deism*), but only such as are still in some degree active, and these it would seem best to arrange, as I have said, in their order of vitality: beginning with those which show the faintest tremors of remaining life and ending with the most vigorous, though already showing signs of fatigue.

In such a sequence there would seem to be five principal bodies.

(1) There is the most antiquated and moribund of the series, the *Biblical* attack: that is, the comparison of Catholic doctrine, morals, and practice, to their disadvantage, with the words of Holy Writ, regarded as a final authority in the *Literal* meaning of every word there found:[1] the words of the said document also to be treated as all sufficient, and anything not there plainly recorded or enjoined to be branded false. This, which is called in the United States the "Fundamentalist" attitude, may also be called, on our side of the Atlantic, "the attitude of the Bible Christian."

(2) *Materialism:* the old-fashioned and very downright philosophy which ascribed every phenomenon to a material cause.

---

1. With the notable exception: the words: *"This is my Body...this is my Blood."* There is irony in the insistence upon that *one* inconsistency.

27

This was postulated as a Dogma, from which it was deduced that not only all transcendental and supernatural but even all spiritual causes were out of court. Those who accepted them suffered from illusion; and particularly so did Catholics who rely upon a full transcendental philosophy, approve supernatural explanations and refer all things, ultimately, to a spiritual cause.

This kind of attack has, in its direct form, almost disappeared, but not quite: and as an influence on thought is still to be reckoned with.

(3) The *"Wealth and Power"* argument. This was the condemnation of the Catholic Church by the evidence of its economic and political results upon the societies it influenced: a judgment based upon the affirmed decline in comparative armed strength and in comparative wealth of Catholic nations, and the corresponding rise of Protestant. This was an attack of the strongest effect in the mid-nineteenth century, and its remains are still of considerable weight today, though manifestly weakening.

(4) The *Historical attack.* This was the comparison of Catholic affirmations to their disadvantage with what could be proved, or apparently proved, by historical evidence, e.g., the Catholic affirmation of Papal supremacy was attacked historically *(a)* by the evidence of early centuries in which that supremacy was less developed, *(b)* by the evidence against the authenticity of such documents as the Donation of Constantine (and the False Decretals in general). More generally the Historical Argument, being destructive of myth and legend, was, by an association of ideas, rendered destructive of truths connected with such myths and legends.

This form of attack was for generations the main assault upon the Catholic position. It was the most powerful weapon of the early Reformation and it remained for more than three hundred years the standby of all criticism directed against the Church, and the peril in face of which Her defenders were most nervous. It began to break down badly and publicly only in our own lifetimes. It is now in full retreat. The reason it was so formidable for so long, the causes of its recent rather rapid breakdown, I will discuss in their place.

(5) Lastly, by far the most formidable opponent within the memory of all of us was that which I will call *Scientific Negation.* The term is clumsy and inaccurate, but a better one is hard to discover. It was that form of attack which denied Catholic affirmations on the strength of supposed evidence drawn from physical science in the first place, and then, by an extension of the methods of physical science, from a minute and calculated examination of documents, of savage custom and ritual, and of prehistoric remains.

Its powerful influence was adverse not only to Catholic claims but to the whole structure of the Philosophy inherited by our civilization, and there was a moment (say about fifty years ago) when it seemed to have conquered for good and all. Teleological views as old as civilization—that is, the conception that things are shaped to an *end,* and exist to fulfill that *end*—the idea of Creation (let alone of Revelation) were thought destroyed, not by a new mood but by positive proof available to all. It was in the hour of this folly's triumph that its weakness first appeared. Some forty years ago the criticism against it was just barely vocal; ten years later it had gathered strength. Then, with increasing rapidity, and for reasons which will later be considered, it began to break down on the intellectual side, fell to the defensive, and has now joined the ranks of the defeated. Some, especially in England, would regard it as still holding the first place among our enemies. That is an error. It has yielded such pre-eminence to a much baser bastard child of its own which we shall deal with as "the Modern Mind." The unquestioned *Scientific Negation* of the generation immediately preceding our own is now the angrily defended attitude of elderly men, who have many younger supporters it is true, but who are no longer dominant against the Faith. It is, though the most living of the Survivals, definitely a Survival; and we treat with *Scientific Negation* as with an opponent who has lost his positions.

## (i) The Biblical Attack

The origin of the Biblical attack on the Church is familiar to all, simpler, and much easier to account for than are most extravagances in religion.

From its origins, the Catholic Church had adopted Holy Writ as the Inspired Word of God. It began by accepting the traditional Hebrew Books because Our Lord had appealed to their authority and had sanctioned it, because they led up to His Incarnation and Messianic Mission, because the first witnesses to His Miracles, His Resurrection and His own claim to the Godhead were steeped in, and appealed to, those Books; but above all because She, the Church, who knew herself to be the divinely appointed judge of Truth, recognized the sanctity of this scriptural inheritance and confirmed it.

The decision of the Church to stand by the Jewish Scriptures was not maintained without difficulty. The documents were alien to that glorious civilization of the Mediterranean which the Church penetrated and transformed. Their diction was, in its ears, uncouth and irrational. The deeds they recounted (with approval) sounded barbaric and often absurd: taken as moral examples, some were found repulsive, others puerile: and the whole was of another and (to Greek and Roman) lesser and more degraded world. We have remaining echoes of the reaction against them including the fury of those heretics who ascribed them to the Devil; and even after they had been flooding Christian study for nearly four hundred years you may find such an ardent follower of them as St. Augustine confessing that they had disgusted his cultivated taste and that their alien style had presented for him an abject contrast to the noble tradition of classical letters.

But the Church firmly maintained their supernatural value and revered them as Divine Oracles bearing testimony to Her Founder. She did not indeed accept them of themselves. Of themselves they would not have concerned her. As law they were superseded. But they introduced and pointed to the Divine Event whence She sprang, and *as such* were sanctified.

The Church added to the Canon further books which were of greater moment, for these were not adumbrations and forerunners but records of the essential doctrines whereon She was founded. The precepts of Our Lord Himself as collected by His companions and their immediate associates, the chief events of His Mission, His Passion, His Rising from the Dead, the inward meaning of all this as He revealed it to the Apostolic group whom He had chosen (and in particular to St. John) these formed the *Gospels* of the Church: Her new and good tidings for men. These stood unique and on a different plane from aught else in the collection. To them were added the letters and exhortations written by the first propagators of the Faith and their successors, as also apocalyptic and symbolic treatises.

The process of deciding what among the books read in the Churches should be admitted as inspired was long. There was a sifting of the older Hebrew books, which left some of them outside the Canon; of the newer Christian books, which excluded some of these also (as the Epistles of Clement, the Shepherd of Hermas). By the fourth and fifth centuries the thing was fixed. Its original Greek version in the East, its Latin translation in the West, had reached final form and Europe was henceforward in possession of the Holy Bible preserved and imposed by the Authority of the Catholic Church.

The living voice of the Church must obviously be the organ of doctrine, and tradition its main support. But the Church also persistently maintained the parallel authority of Scripture. Doctrine was confirmed by quotation from it and a ceaseless appeal was made throughout the centuries to the written text of the Canon. Though no Bible had existed, the Church would have sufficed to give her own witness to truth: but to the Bible, Her book, She perpetually referred. Thus the Primacy of Peter was amply founded in an unbroken acceptance of the doctrine: but She emphasized the Petrine texts and has engraved them on Her central shrine at Rome. The dogma of the Eucharist is Hers to affirm and define: but She also sends Her adherents, as well as Her opponents, to excerpts from the Gospel accounts of the Last Supper.

Therefore it was, on account of the Church's own practice in the matter and the Education she had given Europe therein, that when the great revolt broke out against Her four hundred years ago, Her own teaching was abused against Her. By a pretty irony,

that Catholic thing which only the overwhelming authority of
the Church over men's minds had compelled them to accept,
was taken up as a weapon to destroy Her.

The men of the sixteenth century could only live by Authority,
in religious matters as in civil. If the Primary Authority, the
Catholic Hierarchy, was to be dispossessed, the secondary
authority must be established as all sufficing: thus Bibliolatry
appeared. The Bible, stark, uninterpreted, was set up as the one
and only guide to truth. By the seventeenth century the Bible
became an idol; and the intellectual effects of so base a perversion were not slow to appear. Men came to know so little of
their own past that all the symbolic use of Scripture, all the alle-
gorical spirit of the early Fathers, was forgotten. A dead document bound all.

The worst social effect of this was the ruining of the Renaissance. That mighty fountain of youth restored, that return to
ancient order and beauty and to knowledge, was deflected,
warped and fouled. Our opportunity for a full resurrection of
culture was destroyed by the Reformers.

Of many examples one (which I have also quoted in another
book[2]) will suffice. Just when the religious upheaval was at its
height a Polish Canon, Copernicus, revived in a more precise
form, the old Pythagorean doctrine of the earth's motion, and
communicated to many his speculation that the sun was the center of our system and that the earth revolved. At last, as he died,
he printed it, with a dedication to the Pope of the day. This
new hypothesis—so typical of the Renaissance advance in
discovery—excited in the heart of civilization the interest it
deserved. It was lectured on in the Papal Schools, and the lec-
turers splendidly rewarded. It was taught at Bologna. But the
Bible worshippers were furious. On the authority of "the Bible
only" they denounced the movement of the globe. Luther's own
University of Wittenburg expelled its professor of mathematics
for teaching the evil thing. Luther, Melanchthon and their followers roared against the blasphemy of a moving earth in scores

---

2. *How the Reformation Happened.* (Cape.)

of broadsides, and the evil example spread so far that it even infected Italy at last, and at Rome itself Galileo was condemned a lifetime later; though not indeed for advancing the hypothesis but for quarrelsomely teaching it as proved fact, which, as yet, it was not.

Another dreadful consequence of Bibliolatry was the outbreak of vile cruelty in the persecution of witches. The hundreds of poor wretches—mostly women—who were tortured and burnt, or hanged (especially in East Anglia) during the worst of the mania owed their sufferings mainly to such inspiration. But indeed cruelty in general was fostered by the strange new fashion of accepting all the relations of the Old Testament as an infallible moral guide to the conduct of life. Another was the attitude towards the natives of new-discovered lands: your Bibliolater did not attempt their conversion but their extermination.

For he had read that those not "of the Law" were to be put to the sword, and as for those among whom he found himself he might massacre them cheerfully as so many Canaanites. Was he not of a Chosen Race, and was not everybody unlike himself an inferior in the eyes of the Creator?

For the dogma that this particular printed book was the sole and final authority upon all doctrine, morals, and the rest of it, meant that we are bound to imitate in every particular the deeds and the ethical code discoverable in that text.

It had another effect. What was not discoverable in the text must be abhorred. Thus the word "Mass" is not used for the Eucharist in the text—therefore it is an abomination. The war against the Mass had other origins, but this petty argument had strange force. Everything described by a word later than the words used in the latest book in the Canon must go.

It had another. Images were to be condemned; and art was suspect not only in worship but in all life—with consequences we can see around us.

The action was not consistent. Sunday took the place of Saturday (without Scriptural warrant) as a Taboo Day. Human sacrifice was not adopted, even as an exception. A priesthood—the center of the old books—was abhorrent. The elaborate ritual of the Jewish priesthood in its worship was not copied—rather was such a practice to be condemned, because the Church had adopted it. Black Puddings also were permitted, and one might eat a chicken though the gardener had wrung its neck.

But, take it in the large, the Biblical attack on the Church was the main one for three centuries; it supplemented the historical attack; it remained vigorous in nations of Protestant culture to the last third of the nineteenth century—anyone over fifty in Britain or the United States can remember it in full activity.

Today it is but the weakest of the Survivals, and its rapid disappearance was due to the advancement of learning.

It had already sunk into Literalism: the idea that the English text of the Hebrew scriptures, as published under James I 300 years ago, gave an exact historical and scientific description of all therein contained.

The Literalist believed that Jonah was swallowed by a right Greenland whale, and that our first parents lived a precisely calculable number of years ago, and in Mesopotamia. He believed that Noah collected in the ark all the very numerous divisions of the beetle tribe. He believed, because the Hebrew word JOM was printed in his Koran, "day," that therefore the phases of creation were exactly six in number and each of exactly twenty-four hours. He believed that man began as a bit of mud, handled, fashioned with fingers and then blown upon.

These beliefs were not adventitious to his religion, they *were* his religion; and when they became untenable (principally through the advance of geology) his religion disappeared.

It has receded with startling rapidity. Nations of the Catholic culture could never understand how such a religion came to be held. It was a bewilderment to them. When the immensely ancient doctrine of growth (or evolution) and the connection of living organisms with past forms was newly emphasized by Buffon and Lamarck, opinion in France was not disturbed; and it was hopelessly puzzling to men of Catholic tradition to find a Catholic priest's original discovery of man's antiquity (at Torquay, in the cave called "Kent's Hole") severely censured by the Protestant world. Still more were they puzzled by the fierce battle which raged against the further development of Buffon and Lamarck's main thesis under the hands of careful and patient observers such as Darwin and Wallace.

So violent was the quarrel that the main point was missed. Evolution in general—mere growth—became the Accursed Thing. The only essential point, its *causes,* the underlying truth of Lamarck's theory, and the falsity of Darwin's and Wallace's, were not considered. What had to be defended blindly was the bald truth of certain printed English sentences dating from 1610.

All this I say was Greek to the man of Catholic culture. He could not understand it at all. But *we,* living in a Protestant society, know well enough what it was and the general collapse that has followed. For, with the defeat of Literalism, Bibliolatry went by the board; and the Biblical attack on the Faith, a standby for centuries, has dwindled to insignificance.

Its disappearance in one area after another has been extending rapidly. Men of my age can remember all Britain and America, you may say, based on Bibliolatry. The older members of its votaries survived in numbers till the other day. Some few linger yet: more in the United States than here.

It having thus failed why do I include it among the "Survivals" at all?

Bibliolatry would seem to be nowadays a quaint chapter which the generality of educated men regard as unworthy of mention, or, at any rate, of so little account that it might be neglected by anyone dealing with the major problems of religion in our moment.

Well, it is true that even in the Protestant culture no one who counts would tolerate the serious discussion of such rubbish on lines familiar only half a lifetime ago; yet it must be admitted as a Survival—though the most exhausted of them all—because its effect, in the English-speaking world at least, is still felt.

I will give three examples:

Dr. Gore, a man of the highest cultivation, was lately careful to distinguish between the story of Jonah and the whale, and the miracles of Our Lord. The first he reverently abandoned— the second he deferentially admitted. We must recognize that the mere existence of such an attitude is a serious proof that Literalism still has some vitality even in Europe, or, at any rate, in this country. It seems that in the eyes of men of the first rank in the Anglican Hierarchy the Literalist is still a figure to be reckoned with.

My second example is from a recent article by Mr. Arnold Bennett. That deservedly popular writer is perhaps in closer touch with his contemporary fellow-countrymen than any of his colleagues in the province of letters, wherein he has achieved such eminence. Well, in discussing the causes for the breakdown of religion he says that it was successfully attacked at its "only vulnerable point"—the Bible. These words are not applicable to the Catholic, for whom the Bible depends on the Church, not the Church on the Bible. But they are full of meaning to those who, though no longer Bible-Christians, remember Bible Christianity as identical with religion.

Mr. Bennett makes no such confusion. He knows the world too well to err on the nature of Catholicism. But here he rightly takes it for granted that his vast English audience have a universal tradition of a Religion based on the Bible. And he is right.

My third example shall be from another writer of high standing in our time, thoroughly representative of modern English thought and also in close sympathy with his great audience; skeptical in profession, though as Protestant as Dr. Gore in morals and tradition—I mean Mr. H. G. Wells.

Mr. H. G. Wells has been at great pains to discuss the fall of man, in which considerable catastrophe he puts no faith. But when he discusses the fall of man he always has in mind the eating of an apple in a particular place at a particular time. When he hears that there is no Catholic doctrine defining the exact place or the exact time—not even the name of the apple, he shrewdly suspects that we are shirking the main issue. He thinks in terms of the Bible Christian—with whom he disagrees.

The main issue for European civilization in general is whether man fell or no. Whether man was created for beatitude, enjoyed a supernatural state, fell by rebellion from that state into the natural but unhappy condition in which he now stands, subject to death, clouded in intellect and rotted with pride, yet with a memory of greater things, an aspiration to recover them, and a power of so doing by right living in this world of his exile; or whether man is on a perpetual ascent from viler to nobler things, a biped worthy of his own respect in this life and sufficient to his own destiny.

On that great quarrel the future of our race depends. But the inventors of Bible Christianity, even when they have lost their original creeds, do not see it thus. They take the main point to be, whether it were an apple—who munched it—exactly where—and exactly when. They triumphantly discover that no fruit or date can be established, and they conclude that the Christian scheme is ruined and the Fall a myth.

It is clear then that the most eminent writers in the Protestant culture can still be concerned with Literalism. It is almost equally clear that they have never grasped that full doctrine of the Fall—the sole doctrine explanatory of our state—upon which, coupled with that of the Incarnation, the Catholic Church bases all Her theology.

To put the thing in epigram (and therefore, of course, quite insufficiently), they are certain that we are animals which have risen. They have not met the idea that we may be a sort of angel who fell.

Now I submit that if men of this eminence take the Literalists thus seriously—one solemnly arguing with them, another not understanding that there has been any other kind of believer—there must be trace of life in Literalism still.

There are, of course, innumerable other instances. You can hardly find an article in any newspaper discussion on religion—save the very few by Catholics, which are occasionally admitted as a favor—but takes it for granted that advance in physical science has shaken something which the writer calls "religion." He can only mean the religion of the Bible Christian. For in what way could Physical Science affect the Catholic Church?

You can hardly get an allusion to the evolutionist writers (in this country it is always Darwin) without the same idea cropping up: "The Conflict of Science with Religion." But with what religion can Science conflict save Bibliolatry? On every side the recent presence of that strange worship—and even its present lingering—is taken for granted.

It is then a true "Survival," though I grant that it is on the point of death.

Before I leave it I would like to suggest a doubt to the reader concerning it. The Biblical attack on the Church has failed because Bibliolatry has been destroyed by extended geological and historical knowledge. It is dying and will soon be dead. But will it "stay dead"?

The good fortunes of stupidity are incalculable. One can never tell what sudden resurrections ignorance and fatuity may not have. Most of us, asked to make a guess, would say that in fifty years no odd Literalist could still be found crawling upon the earth. Do not be too sure. Our children may live to see a revival of the type in some strange land. Or it may come later. These aberrations have great power. We might, if we came back to life 300 years hence, find whole societies in some distant place indulging in human sacrifice, massacring prisoners of war, prohibiting all communications on Saturdays, persecuting science, and performing I know not what other antics in the name of James I's Old Testament—especially if James I's Old Testament should have become by that time (as it probably would have become by that time) a Hierarchic book preserved in a dead language, known only to the learned few.

## (ii) Materialism

As things now are, the survival of the Materialist cannot be long maintained.

Explicit Materialism—that is, the frankly stated philosophy that there are none save material causes, and that all phenomena called spiritual or moral are functions of matter—is now hardly heard.

But Implicit Materialism—that is, an underlying, unexpressed, conception that material causes explain all things—survives. Men do not commonly say, nowadays, as many did not so long ago, that man is to be explained as a machine or a set of chemical formulae. They no longer, in any great numbers, deny flatly the presence of immaterial factors in the universe. But when they speak of life or of death, or when they propose an explanation of anything, they imply, often without knowing it, that all of which they talk is material: that life is a material process, death but the cessation of that process, and that any human occasion— for instance any social development—can be completely understood when it is stated in terms of material things.

For instance, they will say that a community's character is the product of its physical environment; or again that the soul of a society changes with the introduction of a new machine.

That Materialism as an explicit, openly affirmed philosophy is—for the moment—vanishing, is due to two forces, each of them intellectually contemptible: the first is fashion, the second is the increasingly meaningless vocabulary of physical science. No reasoning man should allow himself to be affected by the mere intellectual fashion of his day without consideration of its value and of the proofs on which it relies. No reasoning man ought to ally himself with confused thought. The modern man is ashamed to call himself a Materialist *"tout court"* because those whose names are most quoted no longer call themselves so. Even Haeckel a lifetime ago had to put spirit into his atoms and say that they had in them the beginnings of consciousness and will. Bergson, whose influence, now declining, was lately so great, went much further and put an immaterial force at the origin—or at least at the base—of all things. These, and a host of others created that *fashion* against explicit Materialism which modern men dread to challenge.

Meanwhile they became alarmed lest, if they ascribed all to matter, someone should ask them "What is matter?" and they should be unable to reply. A little while ago it was plain sailing. Matter and its laws were thought to be certainly known. Today its definition is lost in verbiage and one hears such meaningless phrases as "a substance on the confines of matter," "Matter as an expression of force," and the rest.

Such fashions and such confusions are contemptible.

It is a stronger point against Explicit Materialism that, though perpetually recurrent, it has never made a long stay in human thought: that there would seem to be something about it which the grandeur of man rejects as beneath his dignity.

Explicit Materialism, compared with the other philosophies meeting in man's Palace of Debate, is like a jolly little self-satisfied dwarf who should be perpetually trying to push his way into the stately ceremonies of a Senate, and as perpetually getting turned out by the officials at the door: but who, on occasions, when the officials slept or were drunk, managed to push his way in and get at least to the top of the stairs for a few minutes. Materialism made one such successful raid in the generation before our own and was gloried in by many, especially among the popular opponents of religion in the nineteenth century. It looked at one moment as though it might get a permanent foothold.

Let me digress to confess a personal weakness, at heart, for that old-fashioned Explicit Materialism. My leaning to it lies in this—that it was full of common sense and sincerity.

It was eminently right as far as it went; and when I say "eminently" I mean "eminently"—it was at the top of its own tree. It was not an aberration, still less a perversion. It was a half truth, squat and solid, but human and, in its exceedingly limited way, rational.

The Materialist of my boyhood went his little way along that open road which we all must follow when we begin to philosophize. Day in and day out, from moment to moment, we are concerned with a patent chain of material cause and effect.

Of things not material we have knowledge in subtle ways. We also have knowledge in subtle ways of the truth that what we call an "experience of matter" is not an experience of matter at all, but of something very different, towit, an experience of the mind—which, by some action of its own, *presumes* a thing called matter and predicates it as a cause. We have to be conscious of matter even before we can make matter supreme—and consciousness is not material.

But our jolly little dwarf cannot be bothered with all that. Subtlety is not in his line. He knows, as you and I know, and as the chimney-sweeper round the corner knows, that if you fall into water you drown: so water is the cause of your drowning. If you knock a man on the head, he stops thinking, and for the time apparently he stops being. If you knock him hard enough he apparently stops being altogether. Therefore, the brain when it is working is the cause of thinking and being—and the stopping of its working is the stopping of thinking and being.

All around us and all around the Materialist are manifest innumerable examples—visible, tangible, real—of material cause apparently preceding every effect. The Materialist is the man who stops there, at a half truth which is a truth after all, and goes no further. All that appeals to me. It reposes upon two great virtues: simplicity and sincerity.

I have no patience with those who approach with grandiloquence my sturdy little dwarf, who is so full of certitudes. I have no patience with those who use long words to him and try to overawe him with that jargon of so-called philosophy into the which the Germans befogged themselves from misreading the clarity of Descartes. I have no patience with people who muddle the poor little fellow up with such words as "subjective" and "objective." I would rather pass an evening with a Materialist at an inn than with any of these sophists in a common room. Moreover, the Materialist fills me with that pity which is akin to love.

I mark him, in the chaos of our day, with an emotion of protective affection. I want to shelter him from the shocks of his enemies and to tell him that, weak as they are, he is weaker even than they. I want also to tell him all the time what an honest little fellow he is. For he is at least in touch with reality, as are we also of the Faith in a grander fashion. He tells the truth so far as he can see it, whereas most of those who sneer at him care nothing for the truth at all but only for their systems or their notoriety.

I have noticed this about such Explicit Materialists as are left—that they are nearly always honest men, full of illogical indignation against evil, and especially against injustice. They are a generous lot, and they have a side to them which is allied to innocence.

Among the Survivals they now take a very small place. They feel themselves to be out of the running. Their hearts have been broken with abuse and insult and with base desertion by their friends, who reject in chorus and with indignation the horrid title of Materialist. Therefore have most of them become apologetic. They commonly talk as an uneducated man among scholars; saying as it were:

> "I know I am only a poor blunt fellow, and no doubt I'm old-fashioned, still, commonsense is commonsense after all. I can't talk Latin and Greek or German, but I can talk plain English, damn you, and that's good enough for me."

Now I like that.

But Explicit Materialism is not keeping up with the world. I rarely discover it today outside the columns of French provincial journals (for the clarity of Materialism appeals to the French temper), in a couple of obscure English weeklies, and in faded manuals a generation old treasured by elderly men. The Materialist has been left behind, and, for my part, I don't mind lingering in the rear of the column and making friends with the foot-sore straggler.

The Materialist will not recover strength in our own day. If I may be allowed to dogmatize enormously I will tell you why. He will not do so because the Devil has, for the moment, no further use for him.

The Devil used the Materialist (though the Materialist had no use for the Devil) for his own ends, between the middle of the eighteenth and the last third of the nineteenth centuries. Now the Devil has impatiently ordered the Materialist to get out of the way, and, like Youth, the Devil will be served.

He has made our generation too grand to deal with the Materialist. Spiritual forces have been awakened in us. We must talk about the "will to peace," "the will to power." "The will to" this and that and the other (a horrible piece of bad English). We want to live our "full life"—and have discovered (oddly enough) that you cannot do that without a living principle—that is, without a soul.

So one may take it that the Materialist is today, after the Bible Christian, the last and weakest of the Survivals. And that is why I have put him second on the list.

He will not have wholly disappeared before my death I hope—though I fear he will—for when he has I shall feel very lonely.

There was a time—yes, up to the end of the '80's—when he was a constant companion, and one could be certain of meeting him pretty well anywhere. The world will be emptier without him, but he is on his last legs.

I beg that no one will mix him up with his more powerful, but nastier, modern brethren who are so angry at having the relationship mentioned. The Pantheist especially abhors him. But he is better than them all.

Should he die in my own time, which is likely enough, I will follow piously at his funeral, which is more than I will do for any of the others.

But when he dies his works will live after him and in due time he will return. He is irrepressible. He lurks in the stuff of mankind.

### (iii) The "Wealth and Power" Argument

At this point we pass a dividing line between the Survivals that are patently exhausted and those which, though defeated, are still in activity and still play a considerable part in the modern offensive against the Faith. The Bible Christian is nearly a fossil; the avowed Materialist is a rare specimen dating from long ago. But the Historical Argument against Catholicism, the spirit of Scientific Negation, and this "Wealth and Power" contention which we are about to examine, are of great remaining weight though declining. They form part, still, of active discussion and they still affect the issue.

The "Wealth and Power" argument is briefly as follows:

The Catholic Church is false because nations of Catholic culture have declined steadily in temporal wealth and power as compared with the nations of an anti-Catholic culture, which, in this particular instance, means the Protestant culture.

The first remark we make upon hearing such an argument is that, supposing it to be true, it suffers from two defects in application: *(a)* It is irrelevant; *(b)* It does not establish a chain of cause and effect.

The second remark we make is that it is not, true.

We stand, when confronted by this "Wealth and Power" argument, much as a man might stand when confronted by the argument that the broad streets and the careful planning of such a town as Washington, D.C., was misuse of energy, because it has been found in practice that a town with narrow and confused streets like Cairo, allowed to grow haphazard, had the higher birth rate.

The argument would be irrelevant because the building of a town with foresight, and giving it broad streets, is not intended to affect the birth rate, but ease of traffic and other conveniences of living; and there is no attempt at producing a chain of cause and effect between a high birth rate and narrow streets. Moreover, it is not true. At one period or in one country the one sort of town has the higher birth rate, in another place or time, the other sort.

Nevertheless the argument made a very strong appeal and powerfully affected men's minds in all countries till quite recent years. Even today it has considerable strength. Below a certain level of instruction it is almost universal in countries of Protestant culture, and though, in nations of Catholic culture, modern evidence has become too strong for it there are pockets of isolated, old-fashioned thought where it has lost little of its original value. These belated people, it is true, are rather to be found among those who have neither travelled nor read much and who are thinking in terms of old tags about enlightenment and progress—particularly such tags as freedom of the Press, education of the masses, and all the rest of it.

In connection with its irrelevancy there is needed a paradox which not all those engaged on the Catholic side of the controversy have heeded. It is, that such example is *effective*. Where a clear case of superiority in political and economic power can be established, the idea that there is a corresponding superiority in the philosophy or religion of those enjoying such power will be inevitably entertained by men. It will be entertained for the wrong reasons, from confusion of thought and false ideals, but—and this is the important point—it will also be entertained for reasons which have real intellectual and moral value.

As to the wrong reasons: The object of a religion or a philosophy is not to make men wealthy or powerful, but to make them, in the last issue, happy: that is, to fulfill their being. If such happiness is to be found by an immortal race it must not be sought in a transitory and mortal but in a final and immortal happiness. It is an absurd philosophy which makes one do that which pleases for an hour but makes him miserable for the rest of his life; and those who accept the doctrine of immortality cannot appeal to temporal effects as the aim of a true religion. But there is irrelevancy in the argument even for that increasing number who reject the ancient doctrine of immortality, which irrelevancy is that wealth and political power do not of themselves produce even mortal happiness. Even if the wealth and power be well distributed throughout a community, its members will not be happy unless they are inwardly so, and obviously where the distribution is bad, where the few have a vast superfluity and the many are consumed by anxiety or want, or where a few controllers can exercise their will over the many, society has failed, even though its total wealth and power be increased.

What then is the false reason which, in spite of such obvious truths, impels men to accept the argument? It is that all men have as *individuals* an appetite for wealth and for the power it brings, and the confusion between this and final good is the commonest of errors. Indeed, to our race, save when it is trained in the Catholic philosophy, wealth and power appear as being almost self-evidently the objects of life. St. Thomas has discussed that illusion in his famous question: "Whether money be the main good?" and all men not caring to pursue the reasoning to its conclusion, answer "Yes." Even where the Faith is preserved men pursue wealth and power inordinately. Where the Faith is lost they pursue nothing else.

Now the *individual,* being thus filled with the pursuit of wealth and the power it brings, projects himself into the community and sees in its increasing total riches a sort of greater individual doing what he himself would wish to do. In that pursuit he impoverishes himself and most others to the advantage of a small number, but the effect is lost upon him in the illusion of general prosperity.

Thus our industrial towns in the modern world boast their good fortune, though the bulk of their inhabitants are needy or half-enslaved.

Such are the false reasons which impel men to accept the argument when, in fact, greater total wealth and power are present in a Protestant than in a Catholic society.

But are there reasons for accepting it which have a real intellectual and moral value? There are—and that is the point I would particularly emphasize, because it is commonly forgotten.

We all live by economic effort and we all rejoice in the strength of our country. Virtue and necessity combine to make us do so. We rightly blame habits of sloth or a mood of indifference to the greatness of the state. When we say, for instance, that drunkenness ruins the power of production in a man, or corruption among its politicians the political power in a nation, we are putting things on a high and good ground, though not on the highest. The highest ground on which to condemn drunkenness in the workers and corruption in public men is that each is morally evil. But to say that their effects impoverish and weaken is to put their condemnation on sufficient grounds. If men hold a moral code which permits such things we rightly judge, by the outward effects of that code (proverty and national failure), that their code is false. If another code produces sobriety and hard word and a strict discipline over Politicians, forbidding their taking bribes or submitting to blackmail, then, *other things being equal,* we rightly conclude that this second code is the better. It is this commonsense consideration that is of such weight in the argument. If, wherever Catholicism ruled the minds of men and in proportion to its influence we found want and misery due to sloth and other bad habits and a breakdown in the power of the state; if wherever Catholicism was expelled, and in proportion to its absence, we found cheerful, productive, willing industry and a high standard maintained in the public service—especially in its chiefs; if in the first we found external ugliness, vile and insufficient food and drink, dirt and misery, while in the second we found beauty in building, good cooking, cleanliness and merriment, then nothing could prevent men from deciding for the second against the first. The practical argument would be too strong for the theoretical. No presentation of truth in the abstract could avail against the visible, tangible thing present to people's eyes and hands. Here things go well and better and better. There they go badly and worse and worse. The conclusion is obvious.

Now that is precisely the ground on which the "Wealth and Power" argument stood in its moment of chief effect, which was the mid-nineteenth century. There, though it had been badly battered, it stands for many even today.

That argument was particularly effective in England during the same mid-nineteenth century, and still remained very effective there to its close. This was a period when Protestant England was rapidly increasing in wealth, numbers, and extent of dominion, and when the nations of Catholic culture suffered either from decline in wealth in one case, or decline in population in another, or internal convulsions from which England was singularly free. Further, the example immediately to hand (that of Ireland) powerfully affected the minds of Englishmen. They saw there a nation of Catholic culture rapidly declining in wealth and numbers, compared with their own. They did not consider their own contribution to this result. They thought it an example of cosmic process, of divine judgment.

It was customary at the same time to press the contrast with Spain in particular. In all our popular histories a continuous curve of advance was shown from the England of the sixteenth century challenging the might of Spain and defeating it in battle, to the present day.

We were shown Protestant England advancing unlimitedly and

the all-powerful Catholic Champion of the sixteenth century falling from lower to lower level for three hundred years, losing its dominion and wealth, lagging further and further and further behind in the advance of material science, failing in population and sinking to what an English Prime Minister, the most capable man of his generation, called "a dying nation."

At the same time, in the more apparently prosperous nations of Catholic culture, it was the anti-Catholic forces which were allied to material prosperity and political power. The revival of France after 1871 was slow until, in 1876, an anti-Catholic group captured the machine and maintained its power. It transformed public education, successfully copied alien institutions, increased the apparent wealth of the nation (or at any rate presided over its rising accumulation of wealth). The Universities achieved their new triumphs under direction vigorously opposed to Catholicism, and one law after another broke the power of the Church.

Italy, from a number of petty states, grew to be a kingdom united and claiming to some standing as a European power. It did so under influences which were at war with the Church. The Papacy was attacked, despoiled of its states and their capital, and thrust down a slope by which it seemingly must rapidly fall to insignificance. A movement parallel to that in France permeated the whole country. Its public education, its press, its literature took on the new tone, and with it a new Italy arose before men's eyes.

All this confirmed the English certitude that Catholicism was identical with decay, and there was added a domestic experience which strengthened the conviction. A vivid interlude of Catholic reaction on a small scale, but startling in intensity, illuminated and alarmed that generation. It secured a small but brilliant band of converts and roused in its votaries extravagant hopes for the future. But it failed. Its chief result was to modify the established Protestant Church, and it was soon perceived that the individual convert to Catholicism in England suffered in its pocket and in his social chances of every kind. He was (and continues to be) an object lesson in the theory of Protestant supremacy. If the convert belonged to a great commercial or financial house he ceased to affect its fortunes. He was not seen at the head of any new enterprise. He failed to establish a Press. As a writer his history or fiction was neglected. As a thinker he might create—as did Newman—a strong effect for a moment: but a passing one. Nor did the numerical proportion of converts to the rest of the nation increase.

The argument, thus effective here in England, grew to be equally effective elsewhere. This was the period in which Protestant Prussia rose to the height of its power. She defeated Catholic France and Catholic Austria; she confirmed her grip over the Poles and dominated the Catholic minority of her new Reich. It was the period in which the United States, after passing successfully through a very grave crisis, proceeded to a rapid increase in material goods, population, and, at the end, international strength. In general also the whole Protestant culture was advancing continuously in Industrial development. A long lifetime and more was filled with this impression of contrast to the disadvantage of Catholicism, and on that account, even today, when it is failing, the survival of this "Wealth and Power" argument against Catholicism, demands our close attention.

Now let us consider what truth there lay in this attitude, and why, in spite of that element of truth, it was fundamentally false, and today is growing less and less tenable.

In the first place we must heavily discount the Protestant culture's own view of itself. All human groups tend to this false perspective and so do all individuals. A man is the chief object in his own landscape, his troubles or successes are invariably less in the scheme of society than they appear to him to be. But the Protestant culture greatly exaggerates this natural tendency, from a morbid self-sufficiency which is to be discovered in all its forms of expression. This proceeds in part from the "Chosen Race" tradition which was originally rooted in Bible worship, but more from a general ethical principle. It is thought a duty, and coincident with patriotism, to cherish a conception of superiority: superiority of one's own national unit over the rest, and superiority of one's Culture in general over an opposing

Culture. You find that running through all current speech: in the North Hollanders' contempt for those "South of the Dyke"; in Berlin's contempt for Vienna; in the American word "Dago"; in those innumerable descriptions of our own institutions and productions which end up with a sort of doxology—"best in the world."

Next we must remark that this spirit not only neglects what is excellent in others but forgets elements of wealth and power in which its own people do not excel. For instance, Urban Government in the Reich is, or was, the most orderly and economic in Europe; but the Urban architecture there was the least attractive. The man of this culture will note the less cleanly streets of a rival people rather than their greater beauty. If his food is uneatable, that is an insignificant point, whereas if his postal service is good it becomes a test of civilization. If his trains are punctual and swift and the track better laid than elsewhere these are proofs of leadership: that the cost of transport is excessive becomes a minor part. If his country leads in the amount of a particular product, then mass is the test. But if it leads in excellence, then excellence is the test and mass is a secondary consideration.

To all this we must add the effect of history. History may be so written that every advance or success is a climax, every reverse an interlude—and history so written is worse than none. Yet Protestant history has been so written for generations. An incident petty in the future of Europe becomes capital because it is national. Everything leading up to the existing state of affairs is a piece of good fortune. It was a piece of good fortune that the Monarchy broke down, that Cabinet Government arose, that the industrial towns increased. For long it was a piece of good fortune that the population was rising rapidly. Now it is a piece of good fortune that the birth rate is falling as rapidly.

The most striking example of this spirit is found in the neglect of the basis of all society: the land. The loss of a peasantry—an irreplaceable loss in the strength of a nation—is passed over as a minor detail. The immense agricultural wealth of the Catholic Culture is left aside: a nation's volume of foreign trade and the intensity of its industrialism are made the tests of economic success.

Another consideration of the first importance in judging the "Wealth and Power" Argument is the secular fluctuations in these. It is not true that there has been a steady rise in the Protestant culture, a steady fall in the Catholic. The very buildings of the past are there to teach the least instructed man that lesson of fluctuation. History leaves no doubt on it.

The seventeenth century—and a generation more—was a period of Material Catholic Ascendancy, led by the French Monarchy. The phase on which the "Wealth and Power" Argument was based was a later phase—doubtfully apparent in the later eighteenth century, and only really manifest after the Revolutionary wars.

We may recall in this connection (the rise and fall of material wealth and power over great spaces of time) the old Mahommedan thesis. Mahommedanism at the height of its power claimed its superiority in the arts and in military strength to be the proof of its philosophic truth. Would it apply that test to the last two hundred years? There is no permanence in these things.

The Argument has, then, been advanced on a false basis. But it contains an element of truth which we must admit. In the nineteenth century the Protestant culture did, increasingly, dominate its rival. It followed a rising curve whose summit was reached and passed as the century ended.

The Causes were multiple—the French Revolution with its unexpected effect in creating Modern Prussia and its destruction of the French Fleet: the great "Anti-clerical" religious quarrel which long paralyzed Italy, still heavily handicaps the French and ran through all Catholic Europe with a violence only now diminishing: the successful exploitation of special natural resources—chiefly of coal—outside the Catholic Culture: the exhaustion due to civil disturbance and internal wars within it. But whatever its causes (and there were many more) the phenomenon was there. On it all that was solid in the argument turned.

But, I repeat, these phases of material success are not permanent and that is why the argument has no final value. Today, before our eyes and beyond question the tide in Europe has turned.

Consider in support of that conclusion the more obvious things. There are the new nationalities—Poland and Ireland—the remarkable rise of Italy, which at last men begin to appreciate: the slow but regular advance of Spain. There is the rapid and manifest increase—for what it is worth—in mechanical science throughout the Catholic Culture. There is the profound change in strategic conditions. Most important of all there is the appearance of the Catholic tradition as the one safeguard against the dissolution of our society.

That society will pass through many strains before it is reconsolidated. Wherever the Industrial system has reached its second generation it is threatened by two mortal perils. The first is the demand by an organized proletariat for sustenance without relation to the product of its labor: a demand which threatens the very existence of *profit* (on the necessary presumption of which Capitalism reposes). The second, and immediately graver danger is that of a revolt for the confiscation of the means of production. Against these two forms of menace it is the Catholic Culture to which men—confusedly—turn. Against the first the Catholic Culture is a defense by its tradition of cooperative labor, the resurrection of the peasant, and the doctrine of private property; against the second by its moral effect in a code which wars to the death against Communism. The presence of Poland as a bastion against the Revolution directed from Moscow is more than a symbol.

Underlying all the great change is a change in the mind: to one who watches Europe as a whole the chief spiritual phenomenon of these years is the return of Catholic Philosophy: directly, in the intellectual fashion of the schools, but, as yet, far more strongly in the indirect effects which you may see everywhere in literature and speech and action. It is witnessed to by the very contrast between itself and the extravagant Paganism around it. The first has the note of endurance, the second of a fever flaming to death.

## (iv) The Historical Argument

Next among the more important Survivals is the Historical Argument. Like the others it has definitely crossed the borderline between active life and decay, but has more vigor left in it than remains to the "Wealth and Power" Argument with which I have just dealt.

First, let us define it.

I mean by the Historical attack upon the Catholic Church, not the common thesis that history shows Her to be but a man-made thing, with divinities that are illusions, like all divinities—that belongs rather to my next section on Scientific Negation; but rather the attempted proofs from history that the claims of the Catholic Church to certain historic positions are invalid.

*e. g.* The Faith affirms that in the sacrament of Her Altars is the full Humanity and Divinity of Jesus Christ really present. I am not here concerned with the idea that this is but one more example of an illusion such as many parallel heathen customs can show—that I leave to another discussion; but rather the argument that we can prove this doctrine to be a *late* invention of Hers, and that Her affirmation of its *original* revelation to Her by Her Founder can be disproved by Historical research. For centuries (it is maintained) no such doctrine was held.

Or again, the Faith affirms a Trinity, of Father, Son and Holy Ghost, as a doctrine coeval with Herself. The Historical attack professes to prove, not that the doctrine is false, but that it formed no part of the original doctrine.

Again the Church affirms the supremacy of Peter: the Historical attack would make this a later accretion. She affirms the infallibility of the Petrine See. The Historical attack would attempt to prove that no such conception was possible before the later Middle Ages.

That is what I mean here by the Historical attack on the Catholic Church.

To note the weakening, in our own time, of this, which was for so long a main attack, is of very high interest. It is, perhaps, the most arresting change of all that has happened in the things of the mind during the last fifty years. Whatever form of attack Catholicism suffered during nearly 400 years—whatever other weapons might be used against it, from the scholars of the Renaissance to our own day, it was taken for granted that, in *historical* argument, at least, the Church would stand on the defensive; and, until our own day, upon the defensive She did generally stand.

I am not saying that the defensive was not successful; it often was, as a defensive often is in any other form of conflict—but still, it was a defensive.

Even before the outbreak of chaos in the sixteenth century, before that is, the original confusion too much associated with the name of Martin Luther, there had been, for a lifetime, attacks upon tradition which derived all their weight from the historical argument, and when actual revolt broke out, after 1517, reliance upon history as a sure method of victory against the Faith became universal.

There were two reasons for this which are often confused, and which should be kept distinct.

The first is the fact that a number of unhistorical traditions and affirmations had grown up as accretions to Catholic practice in the course of the Dark and Middle Ages. There were masses of doubtful relics, masses of legend which had come to pass for fact, and all the rest of it. None of these affected the theory of the Catholic Church, but in practice an attack upon them was more valuable for weakening the authority of true religion.

The mind is powerfully affected by any association of ideas; also men easily fail to distinguish between the essential and the accessory. Therefore, when any part of the practice of a man or an institution can be successfully attacked, the whole of their claims and character may, with good fortune, be destroyed in the public mind. The value of playing upon such confusion has not been lost upon historical pamphleteers who have made it their life's work to attack the Faith: for instance, Macaulay. To reconcile his readers to his wildly unhistorical thesis that the English crown was by lawful right at the disposal of a few rich men, he enlarges on the horrid fact that James II indulged in mistresses. It is about as valuable an argument as it would be to plead the ugliness of a railway carriage in defense of not having paid one's fare. But it went down and did the work Macaulay intended it to do.

Now, the Reformers were—the more intelligent of them—well aware that every time you disproved a myth connected with religion you introduced in the public mind a doubt upon the value of the whole religious edifice. For instance, if you exposed the Donation of Constantine, and showed that the document was not of the date it was thought to be and contained a mass of unhistorical matter (mixed up with what are quite certain historical facts) you shook the authority of the Papacy; and this, although the authority of the Papacy had existed for centuries before any appeal was made to the Donation of Constantine.

Historical attacks of this kind offered a boundless field for the exercise of ingenuity and industry, because popular piety, distortion of tradition, misreading, credulity and forgetfulness had, in the course of so many centuries produced a thick growth of unfounded things; and men's very affection for them made their destruction the more effective. There was unlimited opportunity for exposing doubtful follies or ridiculous affirmation and practice, and therefore, by an association of ideas, weakening fundamental doctrine. Thus, there could not be two complete sets of relics of St. Mary Magdalen, one in the South of France and one at Vezelay; yet both were worshipped. Both could therefore be ridiculed. Acts of martyrdom containing gross anachronisms were used to throw doubt upon the very existence of the martyr, or on the plain historical fact of his having suffered death for the Faith. They could also be used to weaken *all* devotion to such heroism and to make men forget or despise the courage which had secured us in our Christian heritage.

It was not difficult to show that St. Denis, the apostle of Northern Gaul, and Bishop of Paris, was not, as had been childishly imagined, the same of Dionysius, the Areopagite, but of less antiquity. It was still easier to show that there was no contemporary evidence for his carrying his head under his arm. It was a simple matter to show (to the anger of the peasants of

Carnac) that St. Cornelius, in spite of his name, had no special association with horned beasts.

This, then, was the first opportunity for using the historical method against the Catholic Church; to wit, that there was, when the attack opened, a great mass of legendary accretion which the historical method could destroy, and by so doing, weaken the main structure as well.

But the second opportunity, more subtle and far less ingenuous, was perhaps of still greater effect. It was that of denouncing the necessary growth of the living church by referring every practice to the test of primitive forms where these were discoverable—and, where they were not discoverable, of saying they had never existed.

It consisted in pointing out to the mass of everyday people, who had never thought about these things, that something with which they were familiar in doctrine or practice, had not existed as a practice before such and such a date, or had not been defined as a doctrine before such and such a date.

This way of directing an historical attack upon the Church was based upon that most useful of all fraudulent practices in controversy, the taking for granted of a first principle without putting it forward in so many words: the inoculating of the mind of one's victim with a supposed truth which he thinks must be accepted because it is not even argued, but simply postulated.

In this case the first principle assumed was that anything added to an original practice, or any further and more exact definition of an original doctrine, was necessarily a corruption. This way of using historical argument against Catholicism had, as in the case of the first method, boundless opportunity.

The institution that the Reformers were attacking had existed for 1,500 years, and had, during all that period, lived an intense and flourishing life full of fruit and development. But the everyday man who heard the argument for the first time, used to the practice of his own time, might easily be shocked at hearing that such a practice was traceable to an origin not very remote, or at any rate, long after apostolic times. Almost anything could be treated as an innovation.

This second method was easier to meet logically than the first, but harder to meet in social practice. It has never had any weight with instructed men but it is fine sauce for fools, and a snare to the humble.

Tell a man, for instance, that the Host was not elevated before the eleventh century; that the celibacy of the clergy was in violent debate during the tenth, and that in practice it was not universal: Tell him that appointment to Bishopric and Abbacy had virtually been in lay hands long before the outbreak of the quarrel of Investitures, that genuflection and lights and bells are of such and such dates—in each case the plain man who was so used to the Elevation, Celibacy, Clerical appointment, etc., that he could imagine no other condition, would be shocked. He would say to himself: "This, which I had believed to be the very material of my religion, I thought to be also as much a fixed part of it in the earliest times as it is today. Now that I have been shown this was not the case I find all my religion untrustworthy."

I say that until our own time, the strength of the historical attack upon the Church held the field. It affected the unlearned far more than the learned. It never triumphed (that is, it never destroyed the thing which it attacked), because its method was false. But it was of prodigious effect.

There are three reasons why the historical argument against Catholicism has recently lost so much of its force.

The first is this: persistent reiteration has at last persuaded our opponents that in proving a custom not primitive or a full definition of doctrine to be late in date, they are wasting their time. Many continue so to waste it, but the more serious anti-Catholic historians will no longer engage themselves in beating the air.

So long as they thought that the method was damaging they continued: when at last they discovered that Catholic historians welcome the growth of custom and definition in the Church, that the Church is a living organism in which such development is part and parcel of being, they turned to other weapons.

The second is that, on our side, there has been a disuse of

a bad habit: that of walking into the snare of the enemy.

It was natural for so very ancient and rooted a thing as the Church to maintain as much as might be of any tradition. It was inevitable that the institution bound up with myriads of the populace, thousands of localities and scores of societies, should find each defending its peculiar associations. Such and such a shrine will cling to its legendary as to its true history: such and such a population to its repeated tales. Moreover, in view of the damage done to the whole structure in the past by assault upon its accretions, loyal men were rightly chary of aiding such assault by acquiescence in the jeers of enemies.

But a vigorously critical spirit arising within the Church has grown continually and has by this time done invaluable service. It has even sometimes exceeded its task, but at any rate it has cleared us of reproach.

The third reason is allied to this. The same critical spirit on the Catholic side has at last successfully turned its own weapons against those who first originated the Historical attack and so long continued it.

There was a vast amount of accurate criticism on the Catholic side, begun in the late sixteenth century, and continued into the early nineteenth. But this industry was undertaken either without any polemic views, or only in answer to an attack already delivered. In other words it was filled with the spirit of the defensive. We did not take the initiative.

It is astonishing how late the idea first seems to have occurred, within the body of those who revere tradition, that a still more exact examination of evidence might prove in their favor. It was not, one may say until the nineteenth century, and hardly (in full vigor) before the last third of the nineteenth century, that this new spirit appeared. But, once it had appeared, the opportunities which lay before it proved so unexpectedly numerous that great numbers were attracted to the new interest. A school in defense of tradition was formed, rapidly increased, and rapidly gained weight. It is not a united school—it is formed of various sections often at issue one with another in their philosophy. But the general trend of the stream is clearly apparent, and it is running most vigorously.

There are many masters of this new historical work who have no particular sympathy with Catholicism; not a few individuals engaged in it have even an active dislike of Catholicism; yet, the new and more thorough examination of the past is making everywhere for the Catholic traditional standpoint. And with every year that passes, the position gets stronger.

I would give one example out of a thousand—that already mentioned of the Donation of Constantine.

From the end of the Dark Ages, somewhere in the ninth century, this document was known and used in the West and accepted as genuine. About a century and a half after it had first appeared in the West (or at least, after the date when we of today can first trace it in the West) it began to be used as a support for the Papal claims.

The Donation purports to be a gift, by Constantine, of Sovereignty to the Bishop of Rome over what were later the States of the Church and the Imperial city itself. It is bound up with a story of Pope Sylvester, the contemporary of Constantine, who is represented as having baptized the Emperor when he had been stricken with leprosy, as having cured the leprosy miraculously by the baptism, and as having received these new privileges and governing powers, together with a number of emblematic honors, from the gratitude of the Emperor.

The authenticity of that document began to be questioned in the fifteenth century. Arguments against it were advanced by Peacock, the eccentric but learned Bishop of Chichester in England, and by Valla, the great Italian scholar in Pavia.

It was badly shaken before the Reformation broke out. It became clear to the bulk of educated opinion in the sixteenth century that the thing was not tenable. It was full of myth; it antedated the baptism of Constantine by many years, and it was written in the spirit not of the early fourth century but rather of the seventh or even eighth.

Yet it was still defended officially upon the Catholic side until quite a late date, not being finally abandoned until the seventeenth century.

Now here was a clear case of the historic method used as a weapon against the Faith, and used with apparently complete success. A false document had been accepted as true; it had even been used for supporting a definite piece of Catholic doctrine: to wit, the supremacy of the Bishop of Rome; it had been defended long after it had lost all right to be defended; it was reluctantly abandoned, and the end of the conflict looked like nothing but a humiliating defeat of ignorance at the best, and deliberate falsehood at the worst.

But note what has followed in quite recent times.

The Donation has not been rehabilitated. For the matter of that, it never will be. But what has been proved is a most interesting example of the way in which legend and myth testify to the truth of tradition. A much more elaborate and widespread research than any of its critics had hitherto undertaken established in some points the probability, in others, the certitude, that the document first known to us (in the West) as the Donation of Constantine, was derived from a much earlier legend, the acts of St. Sylvester.

It was further established that these apocryphal acts of St. Sylvester were, like all their kind, rooted in real history. They were formed by layers and layers of accumulated legend wrapping up a kernel of truth: as for instance, the approximate date when Papal government began in the City, the gift of the Lateran Palace, the contemporary careers of St. Sylvester and Constantine, etc. Had all record of the early fourth century been lost these apocryphal acts would have given us half a dozen of the most important facts upon it.

The process continues on all sides. It was but the other day, for instance, that a Catholic scholar[3] exploded the hitherto unquestioned academic teaching of an independent Celtic Church not in communion with, nor acknowledging the supremacy of, Rome. Non-Catholic scholars have similarly re-established probable authenticity for the famous passage upon Our Lord in Josephus. A scholar definitely—even violently—

---

3. M. V. Hay: *A Chain of Error in Scottish History* (Longmans).

Anti-Catholic[4] re-established on critical grounds the historicity of St. Patrick, his mission and authorship of the *Confessio*.

There continues, of course, a certain amount of brawling against the Faith on the Historical side, as in the case of the notorious Mr. Coulton. But that does not belong in this section of my survey. I deal with it in its place under the popular attacks of our time. Serious history is ceasing to oppose us. The Historians not of the Faith remain opposed to us in Philosophy—sometimes fanatically so. But the hope to damage the Faith by Historical research is weakening. It had a long inning!

## (v) Scientific Negation

This, the last of my series of Survivals, and the most vital of them is very difficult to define. What it *is* we all appreciate: we still meet it daily. We all know the spirit when we come across it; it is a definite organic thing in the thought of our time, a thing which was triumphant not so long ago and formed indeed, in a generation which has not yet passed away, the Main Opposition to Catholic Truth. It is the spirit which dominated Victorian England and politically, if not socially, captured France in the later nineteenth century and flooded the French University. It is the spirit which was taken for granted throughout the ruling minds of Bismarck's new Prussian Germany, and, though inherited from the earlier and more cultured German States, was almost identified with the scholarship of the modern Reich. It was taken for granted, outside the Catholic body, as the mark of the intelligent and educated man during the "Liberal Period" of the Italian resurrection. Those who refused to accept that spirit were hardly treated seriously. Catholicism, its sole rival, was in its judgment stricken to death. The Faith was necessarily doomed, because positive scientific knowledge disproved it. Catholics were not regarded as competent to discuss philosophy, nor as intellectual equals. The individuals among us who by accident became prominent were thought, at the best rhetori-

---

4. The late Dr. Bury of T.D.C. and Cambridge.

cians and poets deliberately indulging their emotions at the expense of their reason, at the worst either insincere men taking up an attitude, or mere fools.

I have said that it is exceedingly difficult to find a name for this spirit. The popular name is, without a doubt, "Scientific." All that is connoted to the general mind by way of praise or blame in the words "Science" and "Scientist" attaches to this attitude of mind.

But if one uses that word "Scientific" unmodified, the Purist will at once object that it is unjustified. For the word "Science" simply means "That which is so firmly established by proof from observation or deduction that the opposite cannot be entertained." For instance Science teaches us that acorns grow into oaks; that the Hyperbola is a section of the Right Cone; that the earth is round; that water treated in certain fashion turns into two other very different substances with individual qualities very different from those of water, which substances we call "Oxygen" and "Hydrogen."

It is clear that "Science," used in this sense, cannot be the opponent of any scheme of transcendental doctrine: it can have no relation to a theology and therefore cannot be the enemy of that theology. The one word relates to research for the establishment of certain truths by experience in the physical world; the other to a philosophy. You might find out all there was to find about the reactions of matter without its helping you in the least to decide whether the Universe be created or self-existent from all eternity. You might learn all there was to be learned of contemporary evidence on a Man's life in the remote past without being any nearer to a decision as to whether that Man's claim to be God Incarnate were an illusion or a statement of reality.

Nevertheless, it was round this neutral word: "Scientific" that those connotations arose which gave it its effect in the controversies of the immediate past. There was such a thing as the "Scientific Spirit" of which men boasted, or to which men pointed with scorn. There was such a thing as a "School of Thought" connected with research into physics (and, by extension, into documents and monuments) which was not only admittedly opposed to the spirit of the Catholic Church, but which produced in every department of social activity from Letters to Architecture, and from Architecture to Legislation, fruits inimical to, and destructive of, Christian civilization. It is *that* spirit of which I speak. In an attempt to approach accuracy, I have modified the single word by another, and I give this spirit the title of "Scientific *Negation*."

A title, however accurate, is not an exposition. When we tell a foreigner that there is among us an institution called "The House of Lords" we give him no general idea of it. To do that we must describe its functions, recruitment and character. Let us so proceed with the matter in hand, Scientific Negation.

Scientific Negation was a system based upon a newly extended and a newly exact observation and coordination of evidence, primarily in the field of physics and thence in the field of documents, of relics left from man's ancient handiwork, of social customs and so on.

So far its action was strictly Scientific in the precise sense of that word: facts were established beyond the possibility of doubt, and *newly* established. The method earned prestige by its rapid extension of human knowledge. Its followers were rightly respected as men who could teach us a very great deal more than had hitherto been known and who had widely broadened the basis of human experience.

For instance, manifold observations proved the presence of innumerable fossil organisms in the rocks of the earth. The coordination of these showed that, in an overwhelming number of them, the fossils came in a certain order of depth, such and such in lower strata, such and such in higher. It further showed that, of these fossil organisms, some were identical with animals and vegetables which exist on earth today, while others were of a sort which, so far as we can discover, no longer so exist: they are, apparently, extinct. If a man were so foolish as to challenge this discovery the proofs could be submitted, they were patent to all, and he was hopelessly discomfited.

The increasing army of observers prided themselves on their integrity, the minuteness of their investigations and the accuracy of them. These three qualities are the essence of "Scientific Method" and they have been well maintained.

Hence arose a capital characteristic of the Modern Scientist which I will call *"Instructed Confidence."* He was quite sure of himself and his conclusions. They reposed on no mood or whim of his own. They were not debatable. They were established forever by every canon of the human reason. Opposition to them was invariably defeated without hope of recovery, and his continued experience of such success bred a habit of certainty upon matters requiring his expert knowledge. He was absolutely secure. His opponents were necessarily wrong.

So far, I say, the action of the modern scientist had been strictly scientific. But when we proceed to examine his action in more detail we shall see by what avenues crept in the errors which were to shake his prestige.

We note first that all his work was based upon measurement. Nothing was known to him save by measurement, and what cannot be precisely measured was outside his province.

Next we note that in this study there was necessarily present at every moment, in all its details and conclusions, as the very note of its activity, an unchanging sequence of cause and effect.

Dependence upon such a sequence was not new: it was as old as human culture. A man sowed because innumerable experiences in the past had shown that from seed as a cause followed harvest. What was new was the restricting of the study to this sequence of material cause and effect: the exclusion of all beyond them. The modern Scientific Method did not discover the regular connection of physical cause with physical effect any more than it discovered the art of breathing. What it not discovered but inaugurated was a habit of dealing with this *alone,* to the exclusion of less rigid things.

Now this exclusion of all not measurable and of all not physical was a first impediment to the discovery of reality, a first step out of the path of right reason, a deviation which was bound, at last, to render the wanderer ridiculous.

For instance, I am presented the poetic line:

*"And what is more, you'll be a cad, my boy."*

I affirm this line on my general judgment to be written not earlier than 1870, and probably after 1900, and in the manner of Mr. Kipling. It is affirmed against me that the line is of the late seventeenth century, from the pen of Dryden. I say that is *impossible.* I do not base my certitude on anything which can be tested by a metric test. It is a spiritual or moral conclusion, reposing on my sense and experience of language, style and the mental attitude of the two ages.

The Scientific Method is called in to arbitrate. It proceeds to note and measure all the physical circumstance. The paper on which the fragment is written is by every test identical with that of certain Dryden MSS. The handwriting is indistinguishable from that of Dryden and even under the microscope certain characteristics of his lettering are revealed. The ink, on analysis, proves to be the same sort as that with which he wrote, and its color proves its age. The Scientific Method concludes with certitude that the line is Dryden's. But I am right and the Scientific Method is wrong. *Where* it went wrong I may not discover (though probably with research I shall do so) but that it *is* wrong the common sense of mankind will agree. The Scientist has made a fool of himself. He may have been deceived by forgery or a hoax, old paper may have been used and the age of the ink imitated and the handwriting as well. Perhaps individual words and letters in Dryden's handwriting have been photographed and retraced in that ink. I don't know. But anyhow the line is certainly not Dryden's and as certainly it is of the late nineteenth or early twentieth centuries. The instance is grotesque and on that account did I choose it: as an extreme example. But it is not much more absurd than some of the stuff we have had from the "higher critics."

So much for the first cause of error. There is another and graver one.

The Scientific Method proceeds from Postulate to Hypothesis, thence to the confirmation of Hypothesis by further experiment and the search for converging evidence supporting it. This being discovered, the Hypothesis ceases to be called an Hypothesis and is called a scientifically proved *Fact:* a Scientific Truth. For instance, the *Postulate* is made that water, in all ages, has had the same effect on sand as it has today. I make the *Hypothesis* that a desert ravine was once a river bed. My Hypothesis is confirmed by the presence of sand stratified as it would be if laid down today by water and further research discovers fossils of fresh-water fish. My Hypothesis is now called a Scientific Truth, not established directly by the certain evidence of the senses (no one has seen the gully full of water) but by inference.

Now this process, which is of the essence of the Scientific Method, is valuable and has led to innumerable useful discoveries. It has not, for the establishment of truth, the same degree of value that direct evidence has. Yet it is given that false value.

It may go wrong on either limb. The Postulate may be incorrect or the confirmation of the Hypothesis insufficient, and *both are always at the mercy of a new observation*.

For instance, a Scientist *Postulates* that the more degraded a savage tribe the more nearly does it resemble our remote ancestors. He finds fossil human relics resembling in their measurements those of a degraded modern type of savage. He forms the *Hypothesis* that these fossils belong to a society which, like his modern savage, makes no baked pottery and has no knowledge of smelting. The hypothesis is confirmed by the absence of shards and metal in connection with the fossil bones. He affirms it as Scientifically established fact that this primitive type was a very early one and had no metals. But it is not proven fact. It is still Hypothesis and at the mercy of a new discovery. It is found that the ancestors of these modern savages, not so long ago, made pottery, and smelted metals, and that so far from being primitive they have fallen from a higher level of culture. His "Scientific Fact" has gone to join a thousand others, as confidently asserted and as contemptuously dismissed by *reality*—that ruthless enemy of Scientific Pride.

That is a simple example and obviously leads to no contradiction of religious truths.

But wait a moment. We observe already the tendency to accept hypothesis for fact, and the capital point that measurement occupies all the activities of the man—and measurement is a mechanical operation. We note that these are coupled with a long-established habit of Instructed Certitude. Lastly, our knowledge of men tells us that they establish among themselves, in any occupation, a corporate tradition or "school" in the tenets of which the older members of the craft are firmly fixed—not to say "rusted in"—and to which recruits subscribe unconsciously as they are absorbed into the main body.

Put all this together and what would you expect—men being what they are? You would expect that with time a body would grow up of those engaged in such tasks, which body would, without direct incorporation, be bound together by common achievements, a common tradition and a common spirit. You would expect that devotion to mere measurement would tend to create a contempt for those forms of experience to which measurement cannot apply. You would expect that a greater and greater mass of hypothesis would be dogmatically advanced as fact, that when one hypothesis posing as fact broke down, instead of admitting error, another hypothesis would be framed to hide the gap, until at last a whole structure of imaginaries— hypotheses built up on other hypotheses *ad infinitum*—would raise its flimsy fog to the concealment of reality. You would expect that great achievements in the practical application of discovery would lead to such men's claiming a right to advise in matters outside their province and, when possible, to dictate and enforce their conclusions by law. You would expect such a spirit to come in conflict with the common sense of mankind and especially with the transcendental affirmations of religion which no mechanical system can comprehend. Finally, you would expect that, in such a conflict, common sense and religion combined would discover the weakness of their opponent's position and would wreck it.

And that is exactly what has happened. The Scientists came, the greater part of them, to form an unacknowledged international body. Its members—for the most part—took the non-measurable subjects of knowledge to be negligible. Hypothesis disguised as proved fact rioted everywhere, from guesses at the hidden antiquities of the earth to guesses at impossible authorship of the classics. On the breakdown of a false hypothesis, error was not admitted but new hypotheses invented to hide the failure. Too many affirmations were exploded, too many prophecies failed, and at last the common sense of mankind rebelled.

Still more important in the production of Scientific Negation was the formation of mental habits. A study which dealt only with innumerable examples of apparently invariable sequence in material cause and effect, and which neglected all considerations exterior to that sequence, produced, in minds not strong enough to distinguish between habitual ideas and logic (few minds today are so strong), an irrational conception that such sequence was universal, necessary and unfailing: that exceptions to it could not exist. The miraculous, the exceptional, was impossible.

Posterity will be amused (or amazed) I think to remark so grotesque an aberration of the mind: as we are amused and amazed today by the astronomical errors of Ptolemists or by the credulity of tenth-century hagiographers. But so it was. The Scientist proceeded to Scientific Negation through this quite irrational mental habit. "Every time a human body has been weighed by me and my colleagues it has been found heavier than air. *Therefore* levitation is impossible."

The high-water mark of this confused thinking was reached in the late '70's and early '80's.

I quote from a book typical of those days. It is that of Baird's lectures published in '83.

"Every day adds to the overwhelming accumulation of evidence that He (God) though He might, never does interfere with the operation of natural sequence—called 'laws.' "

Note the word *evidence!* Was ever such nonsense? There is evidence of natural sequence? Of course—identical pieces of evidence by millions and trillions have guided mankind from the beginning and still do. We base all our lives on such evidence. But what rational connection is there between that general sequence and the impossibility of exception? Yet the writer of 1883 honestly believed he was thinking when he was only feeling: reasoning, when he was but suffering an emotion.

That process which as we have just seen might have been
expected to take place is exactly what has happened. There are
numerous exceptions, but the main body of modern scientists
has gone down that road, and therefore the quasi-philosophic
position in which they were so assured is now ruined; for it
warred with reason.

It is no good protesting that the True Scientist is nothing of
all this: that he does no more than patiently observe, never
affirms a thing to be proved until it is, humbly rejects any claim
to talk on things that are beyond him. Obviously the ideal scientist would behave so. But the human scientist, belonging as he
does to a fallen race, didn't behave so. He denied wholesale;
his "Scientific Negation" was, until lately, the mark of all our
time.

For there followed from a confirmed habit of unreasonably
postulating the necessary and universal sequence of material
cause and effect the gravest result: the very principle of negation
in Scientific Negation. It was as follows:

Since exception to natural sequence by the action of Will was,
muddle-headedly, thought (or rather *felt*) to be impossible, the
Scientist denied wholesale all that was external to it. He denied,
of course, all the supernatural in bulk: the birth of Our Lord
from a Virgin, the Miracles, the Incarnation, the Eucharist,
Revelation, Immortality—all the Creed. But he also denied
spiritual perceptions. He denied the whole basis of the Faith.

Let no one plead that he did so as an individual and did not
engage a body of thought. The examples were innumerable.
They covered Europe; and even today the Valiant Survivals carry
on. Sir Arthur Keith, speaking not out of his private opinions
but as a Scientist and from what he seems most strangely to
have taken—at this time of day!—for "Scientific" evidence,
recently proved to us, himself a Survival, that there was no Survival of the Human Soul after death.

I have put the Scientific Negation here on the extreme edge
of the Survivals, marking it as a thing which, though it has
already passed its zenith, is still of such power among us that

it might almost seem to form today, as it certainly did forty or fifty years ago, the main contemporary force in opposition to Catholic truth. The reason I include it thus among the Survivals at all is that it is weakening; and by that mark may be distinguished from another, later force, its baser by-product with which I shall deal in a few pages. That product of Scientific Negation is now our chief main opponent, and I shall describe as such under the title of "The Modern Mind."

"Scientific Negation" is defeated. It knows that it is defeated, and it is beginning to retreat.

Let us sum up the causes of its failure, the weaknesses which have turned it into a Survival.

It has failed partly through its own self-contradictions, partly through its extravagances, more because the imperfection of its method has been exposed: and that exposure was largely provoked by its arrogance.

Its self-contradiction: It positively affirmed on one day irrefutable dogmas such as the indestructible and indivisible atom, which it had to abandon the next. It made matters worse by not frankly admitting error—it never does—but by pretending that its instruction had "expanded."

Its extravagances: As in its talk of "alcohol" of which no mortal ever made a beverage nor will, of "eugenics" and "sterilization of the unfit" which are half murderous and half inept; of the coming changes in man, which didn't happen; of its right to control our lives and perform on us every inhuman experiment.

But the main work has been done by its exposure on the part of those whom it despised. They began to insist that a man who said (as one of their principal spokesmen did) "we cannot really know a thing unless we can measure it" was below the normal level in reasoning power. They maintained with success that the certain must be preferred to the grossly uncertain; our moral sense (for example) to a succession of vague and quite unfounded guesses as to its prehistoric origin, and our experience of real things—beef, mutton, earth, sky, sea, love, bread, wine, poetry—to imaginaries ("The Ether," for instance) which were talked of as familiarly as the air we breathe but which no man ever has known or can know. We know the Gospels—we know their profound effect; but as for "Q," what is that ridiculous figment compared with *them?*

Thus has it failed.

For the special quality of "Scientific Negation" in all its various branches—in physical theory (or rather in false metaphysics ill-reasoned from physical research) in what is called "The Higher Criticism," in what is called "Comparative Religion"— and all the rest of it—was as I have said, "Instructed Confidence." When that confidence came to be shaken, both in its own heart and in the judgment of others, the essential principle of the thing collapsed.

Ferrero's judgment stands. "The men of the nineteenth century thought they knew all. They knew nothing."

Its passing is not without the power to move us. Its exponents of that older generation, such as the great Huxley in one field, Renan in another, were men of remarkable stature. They not only had high powers of expression, but a very deep knowledge of their subjects. So armed, they had come to the fixed conclusion that the universe was thus and thus: incompatible with the Catholic doctrine. Today the Survivals of their kind, men often highly instructed, and also highly gifted in expression, are not, at heart, confident. They feel what their forerunners never felt—the weight of our fire.

We have in England many such survivors of that older type, they are in especial strength here, because in the Protestant culture the opposition to these false pretensions was ill-founded. They know little of the Catholic reply: yet even so they show all the symptoms of decline.

They are as dogmatic as ever their elders were, but every one of them carries the scars of wounds received in controversy, such as their elders never knew. They affirm with the same vigor as was common in a time happier for their school, but it is a vigor used on the defensive. The one will confidently assert that the Fourth Gospel has been "proved" to be no work of an eyewitness; the other will as confidently reaffirm the old dogma that there is no design in animated nature, that all teleological conceptions are false and that no Creator is needed. But in each case one feels that the attitude is no longer the attitude of the 1870's. It is no longer the old forward triumphant attack brushing aside a resistance which it could afford to despise. It is the attitude of a man on his guard, expecting to meet heavier and heavier counterblows. It is a defensive that wobbles and sometimes screams. It often has to shield itself by refusing to consider evidence, or by insufficient quotation, or even by silence.

Of old the man who—in the Protestant culture—got rid of a creative God by making development mechanical, expected to find against him at the worst some negative argument which further research would disprove. He was rightly contemptuous of such futile defense. If he were told that his evidence was fragmentary, and therefore inconclusive, he could confidently await a mass of new knowledge, the extension of which proceeded prodigiously year by year. Commonly, he was met either by obscurantism—that is, a refusal to look at the evidence—or by appeals to mere emotion (such as "Can we believe that the marvelous structure of the human eye, etc., etc."); or by thoroughly bad logic, such as the confusion between the facts of Evolution in general and a particular false theory upon its cause (as when a man said: "I do not believe in Natural Selection, because it would have me descended from an ape") or by begging the question, as by an appeal to the authority of Scripture which the Scientist did not admit.

Today it is quite another pair of shoes. The man who gallantly proclaims the old-fashioned dogma of Mechanical Natural Selection as disproving design and a Creator, is dreadfully aware of what he has to meet—and he meets it, to his discomfiture. It is he now, and not his opponent, who has to fall back upon doubtful forms of argument, to quibbling or to mere thumping of the table. It is he who is driven to phrases like "All Authorities are agreed" or "No Biologist with a reputation to lose will deny," and so on.

Thus, in a recent controversy, one of our most distinguished opponents, arguing against a Creator, quoted as an example of the working of Natural Selection the destruction of light moths upon a dark background, and of dark moths upon a light background. Whether this were unintelligence or quibbling is immaterial; it was manifest nonsense. The point is not whether animals get killed under circumstances hostile to them—of course they do—but whether dead and blind environment will *mechanically and blindly* produce a new kind of animal and endow it with new qualities. It is not a question of whether prolonged frost will kill bees, but of how a bee comes to make his invariable angle for the cell with the wax he fashions.

The old textual attack has gone down the same road. When a man quietly took it for granted in my youth that the Fourth Gospel was far too late to be cited as testimony he had with him nearly all that counted in Europe; the counter-attack had not developed. Today he has to read—from his own champion— the final conclusion that it "may have fallen within the lifetime of the Apostle" and "undoubtedly contains much Johannine material." It does indeed!

It is so all along the line, and this strongest of the Survivals is but a Survival now. Would that it had left no progeny!

# 4

## THE MAIN OPPOSITION

Between the forms of attack on, or resistance to, the Faith which are retiring exhausted—Survivals—and new forms not yet fully developed but only beginning to appear—New Arrivals—stand, at any one moment in history, the Main Opponents of the day.

This Main Opposition of the moment has, as I pointed out on an earlier page, varied astonishingly in character from one age to another; so much so that we find it hard to realize what that world must have been like in which the terrifying conqueror of Christians was the Mahommedan, or in which, some centuries later, an enthusiasm for general damnation and for a Moloch-God led to so intense an offensive against the Catholic Church because she defended beauty and joy. These Main Oppositions in the past have all arisen as New Arrivals, all passed at last through the state of becoming Survivals and on to a later stage of oblivion. But each in its moment was supreme.

The Main Opposition of any movement is characterized by its confidence. It doubts not of its victory, for it takes its truth for granted and therefore its strength. The Survivals are conscious of defeat, the New Arrivals are still timid, but the Main Opposition is hearty in attack. It feels its own success to be part of the nature of things, and, to the certitude of the Catholic (which is Faith) it opposes an equal counter-certitude often so fixed and habitual that it is hardly aware of its own limited character.

Thus in the old days when the Bible Christian was a Main Opponent he produced his creed and its conclusions with a

simplicity born of complete confidence, "Your Confessional is
an absurd and degrading excrescence. It is a fraud—for I find
no Confessional boxes in my family Bible. Your doctrine of Pur-
gatory and of an applicable fund of merit is nonsense. It is not
in my family Bible: to support it you have had to drag in Macca-
bees: which I see is not in my Pukka Bible but only part of
my Apocrypha." It was no good telling him that we didn't accept
his premises; that we did not admit the authority of a literally
interpreted text of his own choosing. He did not believe us. He
thought it impossible that to any man this Bible of his, as read
by himself, should not be the final Court of Appeal. Today that
attitude looks comic. But it was no more comic in the time of
its power than Nationalism is comic today.

We saw the same thing with Scientific Negation in the hour
of its greatest strength. It was quite unquestionable to it that Metric Truth alone was true. It was the same thing with the old
dead Deism in its day and with that older Protestant doctrine
the Divine Right of Kings. It was the same thing with reference
of all things to an imaginary Primitive Church.

This test of confidence in success applies today to those great
forces which between them make up the Main Opposition of
our time.

There are three: Nationalism, Anti-Clericalism and what I
will call (for so it calls itself) the "Modern Mind." It is these
three, singly or in combination, which occupy the energies of
Catholicism today in its battle for continuance and triumph.

It is to be remarked that none of these three is a doctrinal
opponent—no, not even anti-clericalism. None of them prepares
in set terms—as did the Materialist, the Scientific Monist, the
Anti-Catholic Historian—a thesis which clashes with the Thesis
of the Catholic Church. None of them has a direct preoccupation
with her dogma. The mark of today's Main Opposition, differen-
tiating it from nearly all the perils of our Christian past, is that
it propounds no explicit heresy. Its conflict with the Faith is a
conflict of mood; it is a conflict following on a certain mentality,
not on any body of propositions. In the case of all the old
heresies a definite series of propositions came at the origin of

the affair; a conflict of moods followed. An anti-Catholic habit of mind was produced, with all its consequences in a myriad social customs and in all the atmosphere of a society, but at the root lay perfectly clear doctrinal postulates which could be discussed in the abstract and accepted or denied without reference to their possible indirect effects.

We all know what Calvinism is in the concrete, what is meant by a Puritan tradition in any society, and we instinctively reject it with disgust as we reject a repellent taste or smell. But the doctrines of Calvinism were not vague ideas slowly distilled from such a society in long process of years. They were formulated *before* the concrete Puritan came into existence and they were the *cause* of him. They were laid down in black and white—the denial of Free-will, the consequent valuelessness of works, the foundation of Church government in popular election, the denial of sacerdotal powers, the contempt for holy poverty and the laudable pursuit of wealth, etc.

With each section of the Main Opposition today it is the other way about. You may by prolonged analysis extract from its moods its ultimate principles, but the moods do not start from those principles. Their victims are not conscious of any such principles. When presented with them, they will often, and honestly, deny them to be held.

The Main Opposition to Catholicism in our time, then, is not of like kind with ourselves. We need it as an obstacle rather than as enemy fire. It is not an armed body, recognizable by its uniform and having for its direct object our destruction. It is rather a difficulty of terrain. It is a number of mental states, affections, policies, ignorances under which Catholicism is indirectly menaced, or stifled, or deflected or weakened in its action on human society.

Even Anti-Clericalism is not a doctrinal attack. It is a political thing and does not of itself challenge any dogma. It professes—and in such of its adherents as are sincere, sincerely professes—to do no more than delimit the line beyond which the Catholic hierarchy exceeds its functions and invades a civil field where it has no right to act.

So with Nationalism. The ardent patriot does not challenge any doctrine of the Church, nor, *quâ* patriot, feel opposed to Her. On the contrary, when the Faith is the national religion— particularly of an opposed nationality—it is most ardently supported and even treated sometimes as a test of civic devotion. While as for the poor "Modern Mind," though anti-Catholic in essence, it has not the intellectual power to frame the simplest creed. It does but meander on, often quite ignorant of the Church's whereabouts, and when it blunders into us its first feelings are a mixture of grievance at our having bumped it and of apology for having got in the way.

Individuals attached to one or more of these three moods, Nationalism, Anti-Clericalism and the Modern Mind, are often led into direct and personal hatred of the Catholic Church because that organization has clashed with the object of their devotion. Such often end with a special preoccupation of hatred which takes the place of their older allegiance, and they become more concerned with the destruction of Catholicism than with the preservation of their country or the defense of lay rights or their delight in that repose of not-thinking, which is the Modern Mind's especial lure and value for weary man. But the three moods themselves are not specifically and consciously anti-Catholic; they are not so by definition nor to their own knowledge. They appear so only indirectly and usually by reaction against Catholic effort or advance.

Lastly let it be noted that our Main Opposition today powerfully affects Catholics themselves. Coloring all our time, it cannot but tinge the Catholic body therein present.

It has always been so. If in the sixteenth and seventeenth centuries, when that doctrine of devotion to one's Prince (now forgotten) was of the Main Opposition, you challenged a Catholic and said, "Yes or No—Do you repudiate your sovereign's authority because it is in such and such a point opposed to the Church?" that man, though holy and even zealous, would shift uneasily. He was often at a loss to reply. He would do all in his power to reconcile the two opposing powers of Crown and Church. Prelates as admirable as Gardiner, Bishop of Win-

chester, soldiers as admirable as Bayard, the noblest Catholic
knight of his time,[5] came down on the wrong side of the hedge.
So also Jansenism, though working within the Church, was a
wave from the mighty tide set flowing by the dark genius of
Calvin.

This affecting of Catholics today by the spirits of Nationalism,
yes, and of Anti-Clericalism itself, even (to their shame!) by
something so much beneath their level as the "Modern Mind,"
I shall deal with under each of these heads. It is a principal
cause of weakness in our position throughout the world.

## (i) Nationalism

I take first of the three elements in our modern Main
Opposition—Nationalism.

I do so because it is common to the Catholic and Protestant
cultures, is everywhere apparent, and can everywhere be understood. Further, I take it first because of the three it is—as yet—
the least overtly at issue with the Faith. Finally, I take it first
because it will probably, at long last, be the first to yield. Anti-
Clericalism will fight fiercely in all the coming battles, and is
so much a necessary by-product of Catholic society that the more
the Faith grows, the stronger grows this peril. As for the "Modern Mind," nothing can deal with it but dissolution. It is like
a huge heap of mud which can only be got rid of by slow wash-
ing away. It will be the last of the three to remain as a Survival.

But Nationalism, in the sense in which I use the term here,
the intense Nationalism of our day, though it has yet some margin for increase, cannot maintain its present energies for more
than a couple of lifetimes at the most, and probably hardly for
so long.

This Nationalism is an exaggerated and extreme mood from
which all the white world suffers today.

It has all the marks of a religion. Not of a full religion in

---

5. Gardiner wrote to the continental reformers enthusiastically supporting
   Henry VIII's supremacy over the Church of England, and Bayard said one
   could do very well as a Catholic without the Papacy.

the sense of a creed accompanied by a ritual and a developed ethical doctrine; but of a religion in the aesthetic sense: in the sense of that which in a religion exalts the emotions, prompts to sacrifice, ensures enthusiastic support: of a religion in the sense of devotion to an object of worship—worship passionate to the point of men's sacrificing all they have, all else they love, and life itself, without question, to the thing adored.

In this it is that conflict exists *potentially,* always and everywhere, between Nationalism and the Catholic Church. In this it is that conflict has already arisen, and may in the near future arise much more strongly.

For there is no room for two religions in any man's mind. Of any two loyalties one must take precedence over the other. And religion—that is, the recognition of the ultimate reality, the adoration of that for which everything else must be sacrificed—is a mood of affection such that it will bear no equal rival.

There can be no doubt that today Nationalism *has* acquired this strength of a *religion,* and of a religion which, in the minds of nearly all men, rivals, and in the minds of perhaps most men, quite eclipses, the religion called Catholic.

But before we go further it is important to define exactly in what sense we are using our words and what exactly is this "Nationalism" which is today so different from anything Christendom has known in the past, and why it is part of what today most vitally opposes the religion of our race.

There is here an ambiguity into which it is easy to fall, and which one must beware of. Patriotism has always existed, and always will, so long as men are bound in societies. One may feel that emotion of loyalty towards a tribe or a town, a tiny district, a feudal group and lord, a large nation or a whole vast culture; but it is always present, and always must be present. For if it were not, society could not hold together. Now, men must live in society; and therefore by every law of man's nature (that of self-preservation, that of the organ arising to supply the need, etc.), devotion to what the Greeks call "the City" must be present.

One may go much further and say that in sound morals,

patriotism must not only be present in every society, but should be strong; because the absence of it is inhuman and unnatural, and even the weakness of it a degradation to the individual: a dereliction in the duty which he owes to himself and to that which made him—for we are the products each of his own country.

But the essence of Nationalism, in its present form as a menace to religion, lies in this: that *the nation is made an end in itself.* When *that* mood appears, there is present, in the strictly technical sense of the word, Heresy: there is present false doctrine, and all the dangers of spreading and ramifying evil which spring from false doctrine as from one poisonous seed.

Now, this making of the nation an end in itself is a heresy rampant throughout our European culture and its plantations overseas in the New World. It has all that flaming enthusiasm which marks the spring of such upheavals. It is as violently alive as was Islam in its first charge, or the fury of the early Reformation. Only, men are so used to it that they do not perceive its enormity.

Let us take a few tests and judge by them the quality of the thing.

Here is one. Modern men boast that they do not persecute opinion. That is, they do not seek out mere expression of opinion and punish it when it disagrees with the official opinion. They make that boast in connection especially with varieties of transcendental doctrine. The boast is vain. Because they do not punish an opinion which operates to the denial or perversion of our ancestral religion. They proceed to the unreasonable and untenable idea of Universal Toleration and assure you that they chastise no expression of thought—let alone silence it. Which is as much as to say that they hold nothing sacred.

They malign themselves. Men still have the idea of sanctity, though misplaced. And here is a test.

Go to a public park on two successive Sundays. On the first, stand upon a chair and declaim at length against the discipline of religion. Ridicule the doctrine of the Trinity, the Incarnation, the right of a Christian society to enforce the practice of Christian ritual. Nothing will happen to you.

On the second Sunday get up on a chair and declaim at equal length and with equal zeal against the country and its conduct in the late war. Praise enthusiastically some more specially unpopular foreigners—enemies for choice—laugh at the heroism of the troops, call them cowards and go on to denounce with vigor the obedience rendered to their officers and soldiers and sailors. A great number of things will happen to you. Even after the police have rescued you from the hands of the mob, the State will proceed to deal with you in a fashion which will enlighten you for good upon the limits of toleration.

Again, when the nation is in active peril, as in time of a really dangerous war, men who lessen the power of national resistance by denouncing the war, however rationally, are severely punished. That is quite right. But if there be any doubt as to which of the two religions is predominant, we have but to note the complete immunity of those who similarly denounce Christian effort as evil and who support its opponents.

The distinction is apparent in many other ways. Thus, when men have lost faith, they are never weary of denouncing the frauds which may arise from zeal in religion. They are particularly insistent upon the stark necessity for exact and invariable truth on all occasions. They never weary of denouncing the Casuists who have examined on what rare occasions it may be possible to conceal the truth without sin. But let a modern nation be at war, and the most honorable of men will stoop unhesitatingly to the most flagrant falsehoods in the pursuit of what is called "propaganda." Under the effect of Nationalism a chivalric and sensitive man will tell any lie or assume any disguise. He will act in the capacity of a spy; he will lure the enemy's agents to their death; he will disseminate the most enormous myths upon enemy actions—and all this without suffering a sense of dishonor.

This novel religion of Nationalism, this making of the nation an end in itself, has had among other lamentable results the splitting up of our common cultural tradition, our general quality as Europeans, into a number of isolated fragments which do not lament their division as an accident to be remedied, but glory in it as a thing to be increased by all means in their power.

The situation is grotesque to any man with a sense, or even a mere knowledge, of the past. It is tragic—a sort of murder of Christendom. Our various tongues are not bridged as they once were by a common use of Latin. And the divisions between them are not a negative force. Their divergence is actively emphasized by every device. The national language is imposed by force upon minorities. In the same spirit transport and commerce are everywhere impeded by frontier walls. An army of men are lost to production, and wasted in checking and taking toll of all movements between State and State in what once was Christendom; and (perhaps the worst effect of all) that very conception of Christendom—upon which the continuance of our civilization depends—is effaced. Your politician, when he talks in terms of nations, thinks of Japan as he would of Italy—one rigid unit in an uncoordinated mechanical jumble of separate isolated peoples.

But how (it may be asked) does all this come into conflict with Catholicism? That it is inimical to the general culture which Europe has inherited from the Catholic Church, is obvious. But that is an effect only indirectly hostile to the Faith. Where can direct hostility come in?

There are two main ways in which such a conflict is developed, or perhaps (by a sub-division of the second way) three.

*First,* it interferes with the universality of Catholicism.

*Secondly,* it lends to national ends functions which are essentially religious, such as the teaching of morals, the presentation of true history and geography (a department of morals), the choice of literature and above all the general education of the young. In this last department, *the general education of the young,* the conflict is so serious that, as I have said, the thing might properly be made a separate *third* example of the conflict between Nationalism and the Church.

In the first of these, the interference of Nationalism with Catholic Universality, the evil is not clearly apparent upon the surface.

The nations have for the most part hesitated to thrust their divisions into the framework of the Church.

It is true that each nation has a national clergy and hierarchy—a principle not too Catholic—and also that each exercises some slight pressure—greater in societies of Catholic culture than of Protestant—upon the appointment of the church's ministry—particularly of bishops. It is also true that in the relations of each nation to foreign Catholic religions—that is, monks and nuns—in its midst there still remains a good deal of give and take. Even during the war there was some measure of exception made for the universal, or (as it was called) the "international" quality of the Church. It is also true that Nationalism has, as yet, produced no formidable schism; as yet no excess of national feeling has broken the discipline of unity within the official body of the Church, and it may even be fairly surmised that Nationalism will never be strong enough—in our time—to create a situation so disastrous. For we have had before our eyes during now so many generations, such a lesson in what follows upon the loss of unity, that the most enthusiastic of Catholic Nationalists fight shy of establishing new independent national Churches. But it remains true that Nationalism has divided the Church today into very sharply defined regions. For instance, one can point to territories which changed hands after the last war, and in which, as a result, the local hierarchy was at once changed, as though it were a part of national officialdom. Yet, I repeat, on the surface the evil of excessive Nationalism as affecting the universality of the Church has not strikingly appeared. Its effects have been slight—so far.

In the second department, that of letters and of the official attitude towards history and geography, contemporary and of the past, and especially the education of the young, it is another matter. There the effect of Nationalism comes in very strongly indeed, and there are already districts in which a clash between it and the very minimum required by the Faith has taken place.

Nationalism has, among other evils, bred that of a powerful bureaucracy in each state: a rigid centralization, and a deplorable uniformity within each frontier exactly corresponding to the violent contrast between either side of that frontier.

The worship of the nation has been able to make men tolerate under its authority what they could never have tolerated from princes: a submission to rule, which, through sumptuary laws on food and drink, through conscription, through a cast-iron system of compulsory instruction for all on State-ordered lines, and through a State examination at the gate of every profession, has almost killed the citizen's power to react upon that which controls him, and has almost destroyed that variety which is the mark of life.

In the field of compulsory state instruction especially has Nationalism come in conflict with Catholicism.

The phenomenon can be studied with greater clearness in a nation of Catholic culture than in a nation of non-Catholic. Thus in England the Protestantism which has been the homogeneous culture of the nation for over two hundred years so permeates the national literature, history and attitude towards all political problems, that it has become difficult to distinguish it from citizenship. I have seen historical textbooks which are little more than anti-Catholic propaganda—the late Mr. Bright's, for instance, and Mr. Trevelyan's—used currently in Catholic schools. The national Protestant legend is paramount. In Italy and France it is not so. There is there a very clear-cut distinction between the tendency which subordinates all education towards a national ideal and that which puts the religious ideal first. There is not only a distinction—there is conflict.

This religion of Nationalism is supplemented by the character of modern governments, and we discover that, throughout Europe, governments (whether Parliamentary, and therefore oligarchic and plutocratic, as in France and England, or monarchical, and therefore popular, as in Poland, Spain and Italy) are either anti-Catholic at the worst, or, when they are sympathetic with the Church, quite external to Her and capable on any occasion of hostility.

Now, these governments—or those behind them who speak through them—have the executive in their hands: the police and the courts of law.

It is therefore essential in any study of the political circumstance in which the Church stands today to admit a consideration of the attitude of the various governments towards it.

We have all observed since the War the effect produced by the releasing of some Catholic peoples, notably the Poles and the Irish, and the increase of power in others—notably Italy. On that side the Church has been greatly strengthened. But governments are not the same things as peoples. Governments are, under a dictatorship, the instruments of popular feeling, and even in Parliamentary countries they are, though really the servants of the wealthy, nominally the spokesmen of the populace, however weak their title to such spokesmanship may be. But in neither case are they the people. And however Catholic a people, it will hardly, today, have a Catholic government.

Further, the strength of governments is still considerable. It is no longer as great as the strength of finance, and it is more efficacious in one country than in another. For instance, government is far stronger and of more effect on the national fate in Italy than in France, for the Italians admire and support their highly personal form of government, and obey it. The French despise their Parliamentarians, and obey them as little as possible. But everywhere government makes a great difference, and the attitude of government, for or against the Catholic Church, is of first-class political moment.

To a great many people the mere suggestion that a modern government may be "for" or "against" the Catholic Church sounds nonsense. The forms of modern government mask its character, and the fashion of our day is in favor of a pretended neutrality in the matter of religion. Moreover, it is perfectly true that (until the fashion changes) you will have neither overt persecution of the Church nor, for that matter, overt establishment of it. Thus, the Masonic Government at Prague, in its most anti-Catholic moment, strongly supported an attempted schism within the body of the Church in Bohemia, but it dared not, in its desire to conform with its own "liberal" formula, actually attack the Church as such; it could not forbid her services or the practice of the Faithful. The only government so to act has been that of Mexico; and even there some sort of pretext was advanced, not religious, but political. On the other hand, Poland, as we have seen, when upon the point of declaring Catholicism the established religion of the country, also felt the influence of our current irreligious conventions, avoided the issue, and did not confirm that establishment.

But though there is no overt declaration of hostility, the governments of the world can nonetheless be classed as upon the whole opposed to the influence of the Catholic Church. This character can be seen more in their indirect effects than in any other fashion. The hostility is hardly ever, save in such extreme cases as Mexico, to be discovered in the active suppression of the Faith. It is to be seen in the discountenancing of Catholic immigration, in the spirit wherewith educational laws are administered and even in the diplomatic treatment of foreign nations. Thus there is no doubt that the political sympathy in England and America with Prussia after the war, the saving at Versailles by the English and American delegates of the unnatural rule of Prussia over the Catholic West of Germany, the dismemberment of Austria, the denial to the Hungarians of their natural prince—all these were the products of religious sympathy and antipathy. The outcry against the occupation of the Ruhr and against the establishment of a Rhenish state were other examples.

But that point in the world where you see the thing under the strongest light is Paris. It is the attitude of a French Government towards the Catholic Church, which is of most effect at the present moment upon the political side of that Church's fortunes. This is because the French people are themselves so strongly divided between clerical and anti-clerical; because the organization of the State in France is so military and mechanical; and because national feeling is perhaps more intense among the French, in spite of their divisions, than among any other people.

Two factors are of especial prominence in lending to the attitude of the French Government towards the Church such high importance today. The first is the French influence upon the whole world through a mixture of lucidity and energy in thought, phrase and action. The second is the central physical position held by France. This last is but a geographical factor and therefore only a material one, but it has its weight. When you read a good French newspaper upon the affairs of Europe, you feel as though you were standing upon a hilltop and looking down upon a plain all about you. Paris is equally interested in London, Berlin, Rome, Prague, Warsaw, Vienna, Madrid and New York, and the lines radiating from that central point to the others are lines of moral communication, the patterns of which upon the map are a symbol of that central station, with all its influence of centrality.

French government has been opposed to Catholicism for fifty years. There have been moments when the opposition has been more intense, there have been moments when it has been relaxed, but government upon the whole favorable to Catholic influence has not been present in the Republic since the fall of MacMahon in 1877. A highly organized clique, largely masonic, then captured the electoral machine and has kept it ever since.

It has often been said, and quite truly, that this state of affairs does not reflect the French people. The French Government is, less than that of any other people, the expression of national feeling. The system by which professional politicians whom everyone despises share in rotation the perquisites of their trade is disgusting to the nation at large; but it is so fluid a system that it is most difficult to destroy. It was nearly destroyed in the later 'eighties of the last century. Had the Great War been short and successful, it would have been destroyed at once. It was all but destroyed in the July of 1926 when mobs began gathering to throw the professional politicians of the Parliament House into the street. But the thing has never come off; and meanwhile the clique in power remains still anti-Catholic in tone and direction. There is an extreme case.

In Belgium, in Italy, in Spain, the tendency is other. But it still remains true that even in the Catholic culture (and as a matter of course in the Protestant), governments are, as supplements to Nationalism, out of step with the spirit of the Church. This material strength of governments, coupled with and supporting the far more important effect of Nationalism as a spiritual power, forms everywhere an obstacle to full Catholic life.

It remains to discuss whether this exceptional contemporary force of Nationalism, of the State as an object of worship to the exclusion of, or at any rate, far superior to, any other object of worship, is long to remain.

May we say that there are forces already apparent tending to its decline? Can we reasonably forecast the coming of a decline in Nationalism during the near future? Of course, in the long run such forces must appear, because all human moods are mortal, Nationalism like the rest. But are the tendencies present today so that we can watch them? And are there, besides these, contemporary conditions which point to a future hostility to Nationalism?

I think there are. Besides the Catholic Church there are at least two great international forces (not to quote more) which are already clearly apparent. One is that of Finance, the other is that of the protest of the Proletariat against Capitalism; a protest which in its most lucid and most logical form is called Communism. Both these act as solvents to that religion of nationality which was universal before the Great War.

These two forces, International Finance and International Socialism, act after fashions often unexpected, and the more drastic. For instance, the big newspapers (and nearly all the Press of large circulation is purely Capitalist—a mere propagandist agent for Capitalism) bang the Nationalist drum as hard as they can—even to deafening and to weariness. But that exaggerated Nationalism of theirs more and more loses its effect through a manifest insincerity due to their unconcealable anxiety for Big Business. They have to bawl Nationalism at the top of their vulgar voices because circulation demands that theme, but they are compelled, in the interest of their millionaire owners, to preach goodwill for Capitalist enterprises interlocked throughout the world. They may, for instance, demand a special British policy in the matter of oil, but they will not oppose the interest of American oil or Dutch. They may roar for reparations—but they won't roar against the ultimate transfer of reparations to the international bond holder.

As for the banks, they are almost openly international today. One can no longer speak of any country as having a national financial policy. Some are more particularist than others—notably France and Italy—but all respond to the pull of New York, and here, in England, the banking system is but a branch of New York's, to which it is voluntarily but also necessarily bound.

But the wave of Nationalism will rise higher before it declines, for there is one element which tends to preserve it, and that is the nobility of the ideal presented.

Here we have a situation quite different from that which applies to our other enemies, such as anti-Clericalism and the rest. *They* excite no enthusiasm; *they* prey upon the baser part of man, and actually warn the isolated and the ignorant against an elevation of spirit. But Nationalism has running through it the ardent character of devotion. That is its glory, and that is also what renders it a peril.

The effect of Socialism (logically, Communism) as a solvent of Nationalism is far less strong. Partly because it is an inhuman ideal not possible in practice (as everyone knows at heart—even those who proclaim its ideal loudest) and more because it is sporadic and partial. It can only flourish where there is an industrial proletariat. It cannot convert the bulk even of this, and even should it succeed in doing so, these industrial proletariats are patchy. If you were to take a map and set down on it the industrial areas of the world, you would have something like a rather disjointed rash: nothing homogeneous; while of single nations, England, which is by temperament the least inclined to communism, is the only completely industrialized of them all. Communism will increase. It will increase greatly. It will not affect national separateness as finance will affect it. But the combined effect of proletariat and banker will be formidable.

## (ii) Anti-Clericalism

I come in this section to a factor in the Main Opposition which has a character of its own, markedly different from all others—the factor of Anti-Clericalism.

It is of special importance to emphasize, to define and to explain it to an audience of English and American readers, because it does not come into their daily lives: they have no direct experience of it. It is important to emphasize it lest an essential part of the Church's conflict today should be overlooked; to define it because it is perpetually confused with anti-Catholicism in general, with wholesale rancor against religion and with the spirit of persecution at large: to explain it because, until we understand its nature, we cannot follow the process whereby its votaries have become allied to the mass of moods combined against the Catholic Church, and have by now almost dissolved into that mass—no longer maintaining their original character. Anti-Clericalism may, in the near future, indirectly affect the condition of Catholics even where they are in a minority amid Protestant surroundings, and it is well to be ready with an understanding of it before that happens.

The subject, I say, must be *emphasized* because of its unfamiliarity outside the nations of Catholic tradition. The ancient Catholic culture reacts towards the Church and the Church towards it in a very different fashion from that which we find in the area of Protestantism.

Nothing is more startling, or, indeed, less comprehensible, to the average Catholic who has lived all his life as the citizen of an essentially Protestant State and under the surrounding atmosphere of the Protestant culture, than this principal phenomenon in the nations of Catholic culture.

It is not too much to say that the Catholic belonging to a nation of Protestant culture feels this form of the quarrel between the Church and the world—Anti-Clericalism—to be more alien to him than any other product of any social spirit foreign to his own. As a rule he does not know what it is all about; it either seems to him mere blind hate which no explanation can make intelligible; or he confuses it with that general hostility to Catholicism in his own world of which all are in some degree aware, and many, especially converts, have experienced very gravely.

If this be the reason for emphasizing Anti-Clericalism as a modern force, how shall it be defined?

Anti-Clericalism may be defined as the spirit which is goaded into activity by the invasion of the civil province by clerical agency.

That is the *minimum* definition; that is the definition of the thing in its origin and before it entered into alliance with the enemies of the Faith. St. Louis can be quoted as anti-clerical when he refused the French Bishops the right to seize the goods of excommunicated people. The Irish leaders can be quoted as anti-clerical when they refused to be restrained in their land policy and political programme by certain of the hierarchy and even by the advice of the Pope. Their picturesque phrase: "We will take our religion from Rome but our politics from Hell" is anti-clerical.

In this *minimum* sense Anti-Clericalism is always potentially present in the mass of a Catholic civilization and may be excited at any moment without reference to doctrine or to the general acceptance of Catholic ideas and morals as a whole.

The more legitimate protests which preceded the Reformation were essentially anti-clerical—and a good example of the peril that spirit involves. The irritation caused in England by excessive Church taxation, the exasperation of pre-Reformation London in particular with mortuary dues and their irrational incidence, are examples of Anti-Clericalism in action. The great upheaval which followed in Germany started essentially as an Anti-Clerical thing which preceded and provoked the subsequent doctrinal chaos.

Anti-Clericalism then, may appear at any moment in any place where the Church fills society, and is as probable a feature of the future as of the past.

But the Anti-Clericalism of which we speak today is something far exceeding this minimum definition. It has risen to be a chief force antagonistic to Catholicism as a whole and it is with that force we are here concerned.

That force is universally present in the societies which maintained or recovered the Faith after the great storm of the sixteenth century. It varies in degree with time and place. Governments now support it, now oppose it. But it is everywhere present, in Belgium, in Spain, in France, in Portugal, in Italy; it might at any moment acquire a renewed power in any one of these countries, as for that matter in Poland itself, or even in Ireland.

In what was for long the leader of the Catholic culture, in France, it is particularly powerful and has held the levers of the governmental machine for nearly a lifetime, with effects of the most profound sort, which are only today beginning to show their final fruit. It was all-powerful in Italy until quite recently; it dominated Belgium until half a lifetime ago, and may at any moment now recover a majority there at the elections. It has had bouts of revolutionary power in Spain, and just before the war provoked something like a revolution, with difficulty suppressed, in Catalonia.

What is this contemporary hostile force in the concrete today? What is this social and political agent now called "Anti-Clericalism," so absent from the nations of Protestant culture that they cannot conceive its nature? So familiar to the nations of the old Catholic culture that they take it for granted, and that its opponents, while fighting it to the death, comprehend it as familiarly as they do their own position—feeling profoundly in themselves the emotions from which it has proceeded? We must explain it to understand it.

Anti-Clericalism of this present kind derives no longer from a protest against extravagant clerical action, but from a conflict between two incompatible theories of the State—the Catholic and the Neutral, or Lay. It is essentially a product of the universality of the Church and of its admitted power in a Catholic country, coupled with the recognition of the truth (so unpalatable to most men today, and especially to those of the Protestant culture), that *the Catholic Church must either rule society or be ruled in Her own despite.*

It is not because the Catholic discipline is so strong; it is not because the Catholic scheme has developed for so many centuries into so highly organized a thing, that the present Anti-Clericalism has arisen. These elements of strength in the Catholic position act, of course, as irritants to the opponents of the

Faith; but they are not the main roots of that Anti-Clericalism.

Such Anti-Clericalism proceeds, I repeat, from a recognition in the Catholic quite as much as in his opponent, *that Catholic life is not normal to a society unless Catholic morals and doctrine be supreme therein.* Unless the morals of the Faith appear fully in the laws of that society, unless it be the established and authoritative religion of that society, the Church is ill at ease.

In other words, and to put it as plainly as possible, the Catholic Church is not a sect, and will never be able to regard itself as a sect, or to accept what is to Her the fiction, yet to others in non-Catholic countries a truism, that She *is* a sect.

The fiction that the Catholic Church is a sect, like any of the various bodies around it in nations of Protestant culture, that She is a sect, like the Mormons, or the Baptists, or the Quakers, is nourished by a score of conventions; by that false phrase, "the Churches"; by the offensive adjunct, "Roman"—as though the Faith were but one fashion in a hundred Catholicisms, or as if Catholicism were a thing split into numerous factions, of Rome, Canterbury, Boston and Timbuctoo! Yet the falsehood is so firmly fixed and so long established here that it has recently begun to affect the Catholic body itself. The position is half accepted by them, though in their hearts they know that it is a lie. For the line of cleavage does not fall between the various groups, Catholic, Agnostic, Evangelical, or what not, but between the Catholic Church and all else. She is unique, and at issue with the world.

She proposes to take in men's minds even more than the place taken by patriotism; to influence the whole of society, not a part of it, and to influence it even more thoroughly than a common language. Where She is confronted by any agency inimical to Her claim, though that agency be not directly hostile, She cannot but oppose it. She denounces such laws as impose universal instruction upon Catholic children by force and forbid that instruction to be explicitly Catholic; as permit divorce; as license foul art; as favor contraception or the mutilation of the deficient. She does not admit the thesis that legislation and executive action, in Her eyes immoral, is no concern of Hers:

that in this Christendom which She made She is to tolerate by silence and acquiescence what is damnable.

Hence the prodigious quarrel! Hence the fact—for it is a fact—that She lies suspect throughout the Protestant culture, and that throughout the whole area of Catholic culture are present in varying degrees the elements of a religious war.

Remark the inevitable effect of the Church's claim to authority (through an absolute possession of the truth) upon two kinds of men in such a society of Catholic culture: *first,* upon those who are in personal practice Catholic but who have become attached to the idea of State neutrality; *second,* upon those who, starting with no special hostility against Catholicism, are yet not Catholics in belief or practice.

The first sort admit the claims of the Church in a *homogeneous* Catholic society. If all were Catholic they would have no objection to the establishment of the Church, to her control of Education, and so forth. Such a society is their ideal. But as it is not achieved; as large bodies, even in nations of the Catholic culture, are, by this time, indifferent or hostile to Catholicism, they are led into the solution of neutrality. They regard the effort (for instance) of the Church to obtain State Catholic teaching for Catholic children as an invasion of State rights. They became anti-clerical.

Many such have I known in Catholic countries, especially among the wealthier classes which had caught the Liberal air of the nineteenth century from University and Press.

With the second sort, those who are not Catholic in their private lives, the effect is far stronger.

Judge the effect of the Church's claim upon a group of citizens who do not admit those claims, and who are numerous or powerful enough to withstand them.

It needs, at the outset, no special malice upon their part, nor, originally, any conscious hatred of the Faith, to arouse them at once to action against demands which cannot seem to them abominably extravagant.

"Think what you like," they say, "and even within certain limits act as you like; but allow others who are not of your kind a similar freedom. Be content with a common system of morals applied in common law; and for the rest, treat your particular doctrines as the private affair of your individual members. Do not propose to identify yourself with the State, or to demand the support of the State, as of right, not only for your protection, but against the efforts of others, your opponents."

What could be more reasonable, or more natural, or more obvious, to men steeped in the idea that religion is a matter of opinion, and that all men are now so hopelessly divided upon it that unity is neither possible nor desirable?

To which the Church replies:

"The fallacy in your contention, the flaw in its logic, lies in your presumption of a common system of morals applied in a common law. There is no such thing. There is no common system of morals. There is System A, System B, System C, and so on, indefinitely. The Catholic system of morals is the only one by which mankind can live as it should live; it is the only one under which men are normal and, so far as the word can apply to a fallen race, reasonably happy. It is the system by which your society was made and to which it owes allegiance. Your laws will be founded upon your morals, and where those morals are not Catholic they will be anti-Catholic. It is inevitable.

"You say that part of your 'common morals' is monogamy. You got that from me. You cannot pretend that it is universal to the human race. And observe that, as you abandon me, you are becoming more changeable upon it. The more you depart from my own special standard therein, the more you break up that tradition of society by which we have all hitherto lived.

"It is the same with the doctrine of property. It is the same with the doctrine of future reward and punishment for good and evil deeds done on earth. It is the same with the institution of the family, with the authority of parents over their children and of the older over the younger generation. Where my authoritative voice is not supreme, there you are in conflict with myself; with me, who made Christendom."

Such is the Church's reply: and to the anti-Catholic it is monstrous.

Starting from this original contradiction the antagonism between the two positions becomes rapidly embittered.

The Anti-Clerical says:

"Since you will not live at peace with your neighbors, we must dominate you. You shall accept our schools. We guarantee they shall in no way offend your particular tenets, but on the other hand we will give these no countenance nor even mention them. The children shall not be told that the Presence in the Sacrament is a fairy-tale, nor given lessons on the beauty of divorce, nor even warned against the evils of your own intolerance, but on the other hand we will not teach an item of your doctrines. We will teach reading, writing and arithmetic; history in terms of Humanity and Patriotism—doctrines on which all are agreed. In private you may add to that as much as you will, but that is all *we* shall do. Our system of State morals, our laws of the moment, we will impose upon you. If you do not like them, so much the worse for your rebellion. If we change them more and more in a direction opposed to your views, that is our affair, and you must submit."

The Catholic Church answers again:

"With every step you take you show yourself more clearly hostile. In the name of neutrality you leave even the mention of God out of your system of education; you are already destroying marriage; tomorrow you will probably begin to destroy property—not as fools think, to the advantage of the many, but to the advantage of a few rich and to the enslavement of the rest. In acting thus you are destroying society itself. I intend to oppose you tenaciously, with all My power, and at the first opportunity to counter-attack and reverse your slow murder of Christendom."

Here you have a situation which could never arise save in a society the great mass of which still preserved Catholic tradition, and in which the claim of the Catholic Church to impose its influence was still so much a matter of practical politics that resistance to such a claim was felt to be defense against an active peril. Here you have the issue between Anti-Clericalism as we know it today and the Church.

I will examine the consequences which have come of this and have made of Anti-Clericalism so dangerous an opponent today.

The battle being set between the two irreconcilable policies—the one which presupposes a universal Catholic scheme; the other which presupposes a neutral or lay State, with the Catholic Church relegated to the position of a private corporation—certain consequences follow which the original authors of Anti-Clericalism never intended.

The first of these concerns the institution of Monasticism.

In theory the Anti-Clerical should leave the religious orders of men and women to go their own way. I do not say that the anti-*Catholic* should do so in theory. He, of course, by his every principle is led to the destruction of an institution which is so essential a support of Catholicism. The Anti-Clerical soon becomes the anti-Catholic? No doubt. It is a process I will later describe. But for the moment I point out that in theory, by his own declaration, the Anti-Clerical in his liberalism and in his passion for the neutral State should leave monks and nuns alone. If he likes them, it will be his pleasant duty to do so; if he dislikes them, his painful duty; but, either way, his duty. The religious are members of private corporations, acting privately after their own fashion, and so long as they don't force anyone to join them or constrain their members by violence, the State has no concern with them one way or another.

But the religious orders which *teach* influence a great body of the growing generation and form the minds of these into a mold different from that which the State is imposing through its schools. Their zeal extends the area of their educational action. Their corporate wealth and devotion, their self-sacrifice and independence of financial reward, create a conquering competition against the Neutral State schools. If the process continues, the State will be paralyzed, its effort to dominate the Church will be turned in flank. The *teaching* religious orders are suppressed.

But when you suppress a religious order, you have the opportunity to loot its property. Under the oligarchic Parliamentary system (strangely called "democracy!") the loot will go into the pockets of the politicians, the lawyers, and the hangers-on of both. This first taste of loot breeds an increasing appetite. Religious orders which had nothing to do with teaching, which were merely contemplative, are driven out; the Carthusians, for instance, from their mountain home; and some hundreds of thousands of pounds more are poured into the pockets of the Parliamentarians, their relatives, their legal connections and other hangers-on. At last you get an established principle that monasteries and convents are to be looted wholesale. Their property taken from them and their members dispersed or, if they will not disperse, exiled. Monks and nuns are put out of the common law. They may not own with the same security as other men and women. They may not associate.

That is how the thing ends: a gross violation of the most fundamental principle in which the "Liberalism" of the Anti-Clerical was, at first, rooted.

More follows. A tendency to forbid the public employment of men avowedly Catholic increases. It begins with a complaint against this man or that. The principle is stated that public money should not go to those who will accept the State system; under the guise of neutrality, individual persecution appears and grows. But there is much more to come. Within the State are not only the original authors of protest against Catholic claims to authority, the original sincere theorists who acted without malice or hatred upon what seemed to them an obviously just and simple conception of civic rights; but numbers who are by tradition positively and even violently hostile to the Faith, and who desire to destroy it.

Such are men who have come to associate Catholicism with opposition to some cherished ideal, as of republicanism, or of the nation. The French republicans remember their quarrel with the clergy in the moment of royalist invasion a century ago, the Italian patriots the sympathy of priests with Austria.

Such are, in one nation, some large minority of dissidents, who have suffered from disabilities in the past when the Church was supported by the civil authority, who have retained great wealth, and who are ready to destroy that which they have always opposed to the best of their ability. The French Huguenots are of this kind—hardly a twentieth of the nation, but controlling perhaps a third of its available liquid capital.

Again, an organization ready to hand—the Masonic organization, for instance—is organized like an army against the Church.

And here I may digress to remark that, in point of fact, the Masonic body is throughout the world an enemy of the Catholic Church and active in seeking Her destruction; nor is there any difference in its activity between one country and another, save that it is naturally more in evidence in a country where Catholicism is strong than in a country where it is weak. It is beside the mark to plead that it has no connection, hostile or other, with the Faith, that its elaborate Jewish ritual nowhere contradicts a Catholic doctrine, that its inculcation of good fellowship and its many charities, its arrangements for mutual aid among its members, are indeed consonant with the Catholic idea of charity. All that has nothing to do with plain fact which stares us all in the face throughout the world, that Masonry acts as an enemy of Catholicism. Where Catholicism is very weak, as in England, the hostility is negligible. But exactly the same lodges are far from neglible in Ireland, and in the United States that hostility is prominent in almost exact proportion to the local strength of the Church. Where She is very strong it is rampant. Where the Catholic body is weak it is less noticeable. Where Catholics are negligible in numbers it disappears. In the Catholic nations—France, Italy, Belgium and Spain—the hostility of Freemasonry is a commonplace, and the programmes for the destruction of the Church, drawn up in the lodges, are available for all to read. I have heard it advanced that the origin of the quarrel lies not with Masonry, but with the Church itself, which, in denouncing on principle all secret societies, has put itself voluntarily in conflict with the powerful corporation of Masonry and must face the consequence. That is debatable. But the *fact* of universal hostility cannot be doubted. So much for this digression on a most important side issue. Let us resume our examination of the Anti-Clerical.

Anti-Clericals find themselves inevitably allied with all forms of antagonism to the Catholic Church: with opposing religions and corporations, with all those to whom the Faith is an offense.

Meanwhile, from a theoretical attitude of neutrality, sincere enough in its original holders, there is bred in them and their descendants, through the exasperation of the quarrel, a definitely hostile attitude towards the Church which brings them nearer to her avowed enemies.

At last you have two armies opposed one to the other (among the directing classes at least); the first avowedly and definedly Catholic, having attached to them not a few who, from sympathy with tradition, support the Faith politically, although they do not accept it in their hearts; the second, men determined by every means in their power—subject to safeguarding some remnants of consistency with their old doctrine of neutrality—to destroy the Catholic Church root and branch.

When that state of affairs has been arrived at, it is win or lose. It is a clear battle between the Church and her enemies: and that is the situation today. Anti-Clericalism means today the *fruit* of Anti-Clericalism: its maturity. And, as such, there is a duel to the death between Her and that evil fruit.

One unforeseen consequence of this final black-and-white contrast is the disappearance of that once large body of men who attempted to reconcile the fashionable Liberalism of their day with the claims of that Church to which they are so truly attached.

These men had said for years that the elementary school (for instance), though neutral and avoiding even the mention of our Creator, was not thereby definitely hostile and might well be accepted.

They have continued to say—it sounded reasonable to them—that though the Prelates of the Catholic Church were not admitted to official ceremonies, yet that was but a point of civic procedure; that the great thing was to convert society again to a universal Catholic spirit and not to trouble about details of etiquette.

But the facts have become too strong for them. A battle is by this time engaged, which a man must be upon one side or the other. And when in the last development of Anti-Clericalism the movement becomes explicitly one for the destruction of the Faith, they will divide. Some will rally to reality, begin to forget the empty formulas of political theory, and consider and serve the Faith alone. The rest will be as frankly opposed to the Faith, root and branch, as any other of its avowed enemies.

There, put as briefly as I can put it, is the development of Anti-Clericalism, and we must never forget that it is present, and will be present for a long time to come, wherever the Catholic Church was maintained as the dominant religion of the people after the great catastrophe of the Reformation.

The struggle has had universal effects on the life of Europe and the world.

Twenty years ago it turned the world upside down over the Dreyfus business, destroyed the intelligence department of the French army (which was transferred to the police), gave us, as an ultimate result, the Great War, and, in consequence, the perilous economic condition of England today.

After the Great War it presided at the portioning of the world.

There was a moment when it hung by a thread whether Bavaria should not be joined with Austria to form a Danube State. But Clemenceau cried, "What—*Another* Catholic State in Europe? No, thank you! Poland is quite enough!" And Prussia gained the prize.

Certainly, most certainly, Anti-Clericalism concerns us all, even those who live in sheltered Catholic minorities under the protection of Protestant Governments and who are to the raging battle between the Church and the world as boats in harbor are to the wild sea outside.

But that battle is not yet won by one or other side. The story is not concluded. What we have to remember is, in all our inquiry into the position of the Church today, that throughout the nations of Catholic culture the Church is thus imperilled with risks quite different from her dangers in the non-Catholic culture. There is internecine war. For in the nations of Catholic culture the Church will never accept a position of inferiority or the fiction that she is but a tolerated fragment. If she goes down she will go down still fighting for a Catholic society and Catholic laws.

So far the process has led to a very disparate result. In France, Anti-Clericalism holds the field, triumphantly and yet precariously. It is done by preventing the women from voting, by rejecting the family vote, of course, and through the anti-clerical grasp of all State machinery; administration by anti-Catholic officials; the imposition of the anti-Catholic spirit by State teachers in a compulsory educational system; filling of posts in the higher education with anti-Catholics and the provision of anti-Catholic history; with the same doctrine governing all public examinations; the checking of promotion of Catholics in as many of the professions as can be influenced directly or indirectly by the State.

But the political cliques which act thus stand for only a minority of the nation, and not a very secure minority. Their preoccupation with attack upon the Church has weakened them further. They have created, wantonly, the Alsatian trouble. They came within an ace of ruining the currency. The basis upon which they and the French Parliamentary faction reposes weakens from day to day. It is confusedly at issue with the average man. At any moment, so far, the whole structure might crumble. But its directors rely upon the slow and persistent effects of anti-Catholic education in the elementary schools and upon the economic policy of starving the Church through lack of endowment, coupled with a vigilant repression of that main organism for the propagation of the Faith, the Religious Teaching Orders.

There is something in their contention. There is ground for anxiety lest—and that soon—they prove right in their conjecture that victory will ultimately be theirs and the Faith reduced in France to a fragment of the people unable to give tone to the whole.

After so many years of their action over education and political reward the anti-Catholic effort is beginning to be felt throughout the nation at large. It is apparent to the wise in its remote effects upon art, letters, building, all the externals of a civilization in jeopardy. It is apparent in the national temper and manners. It is also apparent already in a more obvious form, the loss of practice. I have seen districts in France which might be called "de-Catholicized." At any rate, they were districts where the ordinary practices of religion had so far declined as to be familiar to but a very small minority: and the sight suggests a coming generation in which, throughout considerable spaces of the countrysides, that tradition upon which all their civilization is based will be lost.

Herein lies both the interest and peril of the situation. Parliamentary government will always be detested by the French because the French cannot bear oligarchy, even in an aristocratic form, let alone in a form which has no social sanction and has become frankly ridiculous as well as odious. But Parliaments in France may well continue, and if they continue the official forces adverse to the survival of the Faith will grow; for the official machine wills it so.

The apologetic for religion is, I fancy, better carried on in France than in any other modern country. There is active opposition to the official anti-Catholic stuff in history, for instance, such as you get nowhere else; and there is an increasing volume of powerful literature which is in sympathy with, and based upon, the Catholic traditions of the country. All this means that the intelligence of the nation tends to return towards Catholicism. But how far does this tendency affect the mass of the people? Undoubtedly it affects the towns more than the country. But how far does it effect even the towns? That is the essential question, and it is one not easy to answer. We shall be better able to answer it at the end of another twenty years. So far the position is still doubtful, but it is menacing and disquieting. If after this critical passage and balance between political anti-Catholicism in France and the solid culture of the nation, the weight begins to fall to the Catholic side, the effect upon the political fortunes of Catholicism throughout the world will be very great. If it falls upon the other side and the Faith sinks in France to be a separated minority of the people, the effect of *that* will not be confined to France either. It will be felt throughout the world.

For it is an invariable rule in the history of our race that the spiritual direction of the Gauls should be an index of general movements outside of their boundaries. They determine the triumph of the Trinitarians. They enlarge the Papacy. They gave Calvinism to the world and with it the core of dissension. In the struggle of the Reformation they were at one moment far nearer losing tradition than was Britain. Their recovery of the Faith determined—humanly speaking—the survival of religion. Their enthusiasm for the revolutionary trend transformed all Europe. Their effect on thought and action remains. Though it be negative and an example of decline, that decline will color all our world. Therein lies the intense, the perilous interests of the French scene. France determines, or at least chiefly influences; and so far France lies in the balance.

But a survey of the Catholic culture as a whole very strongly supports the repeated epigram of the last years, that "the tide has turned in Europe."

In Spain and Italy, with vigorous efforts, the Anti-Clerical advance has been checked, and by this time reversed. The thing was done first long ago in Spain, and was more directly religious there. If the happy destruction of the Parliamentary oligarchy in that country has confirmed the good tendency, we may be fairly certain that whatever military struggles a monarchic system brings in its train, the politicians at least will not trouble Spain again, and with that sort absent Anti-Clericalism droops; for a Parliamentary clique is its necessary agent.

As all the world knows, the thing has been done even more thoroughly in Italy. It is there rather connected with a general civil policy than with any special preoccupation with religion, but reaction towards religion is strong and fully supported. It is particularly to be noted that the Masonic Corporation is, for the first time in history, subjected to the general law against secret societies and prevented from acting as one. As a consequence, Anti-Clericalism, the very note of all official action between the creation of modern Italy and the Great War, is stricken with the palsy.

It does not follow that new and difficult perils may not there arise for the Faith. But they will hardly arise from the old Anti-Clerical side. It seems to be finally and definitely defeated.

Spain and Italy stand in our day both of them emancipated from one great evil of their past; in both those countries the reaction against Anti-Clericalism is successful and established.

In Poland Anti-Clericalism has not gathered momentum; to the traveller it is hardly apparent, though it is potentially present and a few powerful individuals are certainly sympathetic with it. The past of the country, its crucifixion at the hands of Prussia and Russia (in each case with hatred of the Catholic Church for a main motive), has identified the religion, so far, with the nation, and that effect remains.

It is perhaps the same with Anti-Clericalism in Ireland. Though there, of course, there is a much larger anti-Catholic body than in Poland. Anti-Clericalism proper would seem not yet to have attained any corporate being. As in Poland, the forces of nationalism and the effect of recently past history strongly support the Faith. The citizens of both those recently emancipated countries would, I think, in general proclaim the impossibility of any strong Anti-Clericalism among them in the near future—but beyond that judgment a foreigner cannot go.

## (iii) The Modern Mind

The third and far the most formidable element of Main Opposition to the Faith today, is what I propose to call by its own self-appointed and most misleading title: *"The Modern Mind."* How misleading and false that title is, I will discuss in a moment, premising here, that I adopt it only because terms are necessary to discussion, and this is the admitted and well-known term ready to hand. Were I to invent a new one, I should hamper my argument, for it would be unfamiliar.

We note that it acts in a fashion wholly negative. It is not an attack, but a resistance. It does not, like Anti-Clericalism, exercise an active effect opposed to religion, nor, like Nationalism, substitute a strong counter-emotion which tends to supplant religion. It rather renders religion unintelligible. Its effect on religion is like that of an opiate on the power of analysis. It dulls the faculty of appreciation, and blocks the entry of the Faith. Hence its power.

We further note that it is of far more effect in the Protestant than in the Catholic culture, though common to both. In the former it is discovered higher up in the intellectual and social scale than in the latter, and is very widespread. In the latter it is more restricted in area and less accepted by the educated classes.

But everywhere it is of the same character, and everywhere, so far as its influence extends, it fills with despair those who attempt to deal with its fearful incapacities. . . . And even before they can deal with it at all, they are brought up against the absence of a language to effect their end.

For, indeed, we are met at the outset of this, perhaps the most important section of our enquiry, by a difficulty which was not known in any other time than ours: that difficulty to which I have alluded, that this chief adverse condition we have to examine has no suitable name. There is no fixed term or definition for that major factor in our present difficulties, the spirit which is everywhere a main adversary of the Catholic Church, and peculiar to our generation. Many a name has been attempted, none has been found satisfactory; and there is legitimate complaint against all those which have hitherto been loosely used for the thing in question.

That mood running through the lower masses of the modern world, of wide influence, therefore, in Europe and America, and rapidly spreading to the travelled or westernized in the Mahommedan and pagan cultures, is baffling to label.

That name which its own victims use (and which I here adopt), the "Modern Mind" (or "Modern Thought"), is a misnomer, because it ignorantly begs the question of universality. It presupposes that those suffering from the disease are the mass of our contemporaries and those free from it a negligible exception.

Of course, it is not so. Most modern men do not feel this spirit. No Catholic feels it—at least, no Catholic who cares to remain orthodox. The greater part of really cultivated men out-

side the Catholic Church despise it; and everything traditional
and solid in our civilization, notably, the peasantry of agricultural countries, leaves it to one side.

Nevertheless, as it is the word its own votaries use, I will here
call it by that name—but in inverted commas. I will speak of
it as the "Modern Mind," but emphasizing continually as I do
so the falsity of the term.

If we call it (as some do) "realism," we are confused by the
use of that term with a precise and profound meaning in true
philosophy (where it signifies the Reality of Ideas—as opposed
to Nominalism); we are also confronted by the disturbing fact
that, even in the conversational sense of the word, the spirit of
which I speak is the very opposite of recognizing the real world.
It is a spirit all print and tags, all soaked in ready-made phrases
which have been swallowed whole, without the least examination, by minds incapable of criticism.

Were we to call it "Modernism," we should be nearer the
mark, but unfortunately that word has already been assigned to
a definite theological school of error, whereas the spirit of which
I speak is something far more extended, vaguer and, indeed,
of more effect; for Modernism in the technical sense of the word
is pretty well dead, but the spirit of which I speak is very much
with us.*

---

\* Unfortunately, the heresy of Modernism has arisen again in the years since
the Second Vatican Council (1962-1965). Modernism had seemingly been
effectively destroyed in the early 20th Century by the vigorous efforts of
Pope St. Pius X (1903-1914), who called it "the synthesis of all heresies."
However, Modernism had actually gone quiescent, awaiting a more favorable
time to re-emerge—which occurred in the 1960's, especially after Vatican
Council II. Since then it has grown pretty much unimpeded. In Modernist
thought, all religions, including Catholicism, are based on the inner
experience of man, rather than on objective truths. In Modernist practice,
Catholic dogmatic formulas may be retained, but their *meaning* is understood
by the Modernist as adapted to the religious experience of the individual
believer. Thus, a Modernist can say with perfect ease, "If it is not 'true
for me,' it is not true." Therefore, according to Modernists, Catholic faith
can differ radically from age to age and from believer to believer, which
is diametrically opposed to Catholic teaching, which holds that truths are

We all know the thing. It is the spirit which tells us, on hearing any affirmation or hypothesis not within its own limited experience, that the affirmation or hypothesis *must* be false. It is the spirit especially prone to take for granted the falsity of an unfamiliar idea if that idea is known to have been familiar in the past. It is the spirit which confuses development in complexity with the growth of good and the process of time with a process of betterment. It is the spirit which appeals, as to a final authority, to whatever has last been said in a matter: "the latest authority." It is the spirit which has lost acquaintance with logical form and is too supine to reason. It is the spirit which lives on bad science and worse history at third hand. It is the spirit, not of the populace or of the scholars, but of the half-educated.

What may be the causes of this philosophical disease—and it is an appalling one—which is affecting such large numbers in our time, I shall consider later. Here I propose first to analyze its character.

Upon dissecting it we discover the "Modern Mind" to contain three main ingredients and to combine them through the force of one principle. Its three ingredients are pride, ignorance, and intellectual sloth; their unifying principle is a blind acceptance of authority not based on reason.

Pride causes those who suffer from this disease to regard whatever they think they have learned, whatever they have absorbed, through no matter how absurd a channel, as absolute and sufficient.

Ignorance forbids them to know with any thoroughness what men have discovered about these things in the past, and how certainly.

Intellectual sloth forbids them to examine an argument, or even to appreciate the implications of their own assertions.

With most men who are thus afflicted the thing is not so much

---

based on objective reality and are true for all time and for all ages. Obviously, Modernism leaves nothing of Catholicism but the name, and according to Pope St. Pius X, it is a sure path to atheism.—*Editor,* 1992.

a mixture of these vices as the mere following of a fashion; but these vices lie at the root of the mental process in question.

As to the principle of blindly accepting an authority not based on reason, it runs through the whole base affair and binds it into one: Fashion, Print, Iteration, are the commanders abjectly obeyed and trusted.

Let us take a leading test: the attitude taken by the "Modern Mind" towards the supernatural—the shrine, the inhabiting spirit, and, particularly, towards miracle.

Witness has been borne to a certain marvel, a thing outside ordinary experience. The spirit of which I speak will deny, not the actual occurrence upon this or that good intellectual ground (as of insufficient evidence, or what not), but the very possibility of the marvel. And it will repose that denial upon something presumed with regard to the physical universe, which presumption it accepts as intelligently as a fetish worshipper will accept his African idol. It will tell you that a mumbo-jumbo which it calls "Science" has achieved in the knowledge of reality—or whatever lies behind the phenomena of matter—a final apprehension which in fact Physical Science never has achieved, and never can; because such apprehension cannot be attained by man's measurements and observations of the phenomena alone. And note that this spirit is removed by depths from that old and grander, now disappearing thing, the true "Scientific Negation" of a lifetime ago. *That* proceeded from men who abused knowledge, but who had knowledge and who possessed a philosophical method. *This* proceeds from mere assertion based on something hurriedly read or heard.

Again, this spirit, this "Modern Mind," will refer to all transcendental belief in terms which imply the inferiority of the past to the present—that is, of other people's epochs to the vain man's own epoch. It will call such faith "reactionary," or "medieval," or "exploded"; it will tell you that the Creed belongs to "an uncritical age," and in saying so it will show its own ignorance of all that vast mass of intellectual work with which the past of Europe was filled, and of the almost equal mass of high modern work in defense of supernatural experience.

The color in which the whole of the "Modern Mind" is dyed is essentially stupidity: it will not *think*—and that is a very strange weakness for anything which calls itself a "mind"!

If it were an active enemy, its lack of reason would be a weakness: being (alas!) not active, but a passive obstacle, like a bog, it is none the weaker for being thus irrational.

I have said that its unifying principle was the acceptation of false authority: blind faith divorced from reason. The "Modern Mind" takes for granted without examination a number of first principles—as, for instance, that there is a regular progress from worse to better in the centuries of human experience, or that parliamentary oligarchies are democratic, or that democracy is obviously the best form of human government, or that the object of human effort is money and that the word "success" means the accumulation of wealth. Having taken these things for granted, without examination, it goes ahead cheerfully under the illusion that its opponents have the same ideas. What is more, it betrays that extraordinary ability for disbelieving the evidence of one's own senses which is the mark of unintelligent fanaticism. It will gaze upon that most hideous of human prospects, the industrial town, and compare it favorably with a medieval city—Huddersfield with Siena. It will call a society wealthy when a great part of its inhabitants are half starving; it will believe any new hypothesis in physical science to be ascertained fact, though it has assisted at the destruction of half-a-dozen other such hypotheses within the last fifty years.

I have said that this odd habit of preferring long words picked up in the newspapers to the evidence of one's own senses is essentially *fanatical,* and indeed the hold of this mood may be seen in the singular phenomenon that the certitudes of the "Modern Mind" seem to vary in inverse proportion to the direct sensible evidence available.

For instance, its victims will be far more sure of the existence of vitamins than they are of a nasty taste in chemical beer. They will be far more sure of electrons than of fresh eggs; and when the electron or the vitamin bursts in its turn, tomorrow or the day after, and is supplanted by the What-not, they will accept the What-not with equal simplicity and fervor.

Why is this mood so dangerous to the Catholic Church? That patently it is so, we see. It inhibits men from so much as understanding what the Faith may be, and bars the action of a true authority by the unquestioned acceptation of false; we can see it doing that every day before our eyes.

But in what, we may ask, is it a peril? It is a peril because true faith is based upon reason, and whatever denies or avoids reason imperils Catholicism. There is nothing more inimical to the Faith than this abandonment of thought, this dependence upon a great number of fixed postulates which men have not examined, but have accepted upon mere printed affirmation, and by the brute effect of repetition.

Well, then, the "Modern Mind" is essentially opposed to Catholic action because it is unreasoning: but why so powerful? Why should this spirit, however strong to move the indignation of the wise or the impatience of the commonsense populace, have also such special weight with the more shallow of our time?

I think the explanation lies in the fact that the dupes of this fashion believe it to be based upon evident proof which the least capable could, if he chose, test for himself.

Here I must introduce the last consideration which may complete our understanding of the unpleasant thing: I mean, a consideration of its origins.

The "Modern Mind" is the dregs of certain much nobler forces of the past, some of which still drag on as Survivals, others of which are dead. It is the base product of a better ancestry.

By one line it descends as a degraded bastard from that high Scientific Negation of a generation now passing: the Survival we have already examined. By another, it derives, ludicrously enough, from the clear-headed Skeptical Rationalists. By another from the great republicans of the eighteenth century. In its puerile metaphysic it is but misunderstanding the strong scientific agnostics of the past.

The "Modern Mind" is confirmed in its folly by the fixed idea that someone or other somewhere "proved" its errors to be truths and that the proof was final and obvious.

This attitude of the "Modern Mind" is due to that great advance in those forms of knowledge which are based, as we saw in the matter of the old "Scientific Negation," on exact measurement; the physical sciences and the close examination of documents.

Of such measurements we make today many thousands where our fathers not a hundred years ago made but a score. The practice has given us a novel and astonishing collection of powers over the physical universe, and not a few (though much more doubtful) discoveries upon the nature and origin of classical and medieval texts. At the same time, abused, it can without a doubt paralyze intelligence, and the "Modern Mind" is the poor product of its abuse; or rather, the confused memory of an abuse committed by greater men, immensely superior to it. So the "Modern Mind," when it undertakes any activity—which is not often—confines itself to Physical Science.

Anyone can measure accurately over and over again; anyone can catalogue points in a document or carry on a series of experiments. It needs no effort of the intelligence. So, when the results are reaped, the fallacy is easily entertained that because so much can be done without the use of the reason, therefore the reason may be despised. At the same time, the habit of proof by minute and exact measurement deadens the sense of proof by other methods, and, as we are unhappily aware when we look around us, it paralyzes the sense of beauty.

In themselves the habits necessary to an expansion in physical science are admirable, for they are instruments in the noble search after truth, and in that discovery of reality which is the chief business of mankind. But when they are isolated and take a false place of their own to the exclusion of the higher powers of the soul, they may inflict mortal injury.

Such injury has been inflicted in the class of which I speak. A stratum neither of the people nor of the humanists, but somewhere in between, has come, especially in our chaotic industrial towns, to believe that repeated and certain experiment producing proof of regular material sequence applies not only (as it does) to physical science, but to all things. They are the heirs of the high scientific despair of older days; but the unworthy and illiterate heirs. They make no reservations. They attempt no coordinated system. They simply believe.

They have further come to hold, vaguely but firmly, that sundry men whose names they hear quoted are infallible authorities, because they are said to have "discovered" this, that, and the other. Hence is it today that whether you are discussing the authenticity of a Gospel or Greek poem, the excellence of a picture, or the greatness of a nation, you find yourself presented by such men, at best, with statistics commonly irrelevant, or, at the worst, with the mere name of some man competent in his own sphere, but in the sphere under debate quite incompetent.

To all this the "Modern Mind" has added an ethic of whose origin it never heard, but which has for its author Comte. It is the worship of Humanity, and of Humanity mortal. That is good which makes men happier here—or looks as though it might; and happier, not mainly through the satisfaction of justice nor even by a search for beauty, but in seeking things much more tangible and perishable; mainly of the body. And this worship of ourselves in the place of God is heavily reinforced by Nationalism on the one hand, by the Communist cry for economic equality on the other.

Much else enters into the formation of the "Modern Mind"...It is the dregs of that too simple creed launched or confirmed by the French philosophers of the Encyclopedia. It is the dregs of that German Monism and that German Pantheism which so much affected the nineteenth century. It is the dregs of fatigue in an overcomplex civilization; and it suffers the organized propagation of myth, especially in the matter of man's unknown origins. But in the main the source of this modern disease is the false application of mechanical methods, inapplicable to higher spheres of thought, which it couples with that ethic of Positivism, the worship of Humanity.

Such are the *sources*. But the "Modern Mind" is far from its sources and settled into something much lower than the dead or dying ideas from which it drew its own lack of ideas; much less than the philosophies on which it bases its lack of philosophy.

Note in connection with the "Modern Mind" its inability to state its own position.

The old-fashioned Agnostic laid down definitely a dogma, and a dogma worth listening to. He said: "There may be Something. On the whole I think there is Something; but we cannot know what it is. The organs by which alone we can *know* anything tell us nothing about that Something, so let us, like honest men, proclaim our ignorance of that Something."

The pure skeptic had a somewhat different position, and on the whole, a better one. He said: "How do we *know* anything? We cannot even affirm our own selves; for personality it is a variable thing, a function of time and memory, mysteries no man can sound. Let us not pretend to know anything at all."

The day of such honest men is past, or they are dwindled to a little band. Those who oppose the Faith today as devotees of "The Modern Mind" cannot tell us what they themselves believe. After we have made every allowance for the natural desire to shirk the consequences of unbelief, or not to lose income, it remains a wonder that they cannot tell us what they believe.

And this applies not to them alone, but also to the better minds who stoop to flatter them. Read this:

"The real trend of religion among the younger generation is away from dogmatic and institutional Christianity, and towards an individual and personal faith resting not on authority but on experience....The new Protestantism is not relativist in the objects of its faith; it believes that truth is absolute, and that God is unchanging. But it accepts the necessity of growth and change in our beliefs...We must sit very loose to tradition, and keep our minds open. Our anchor is what used to be called the testimony of the Holy Spirit, which assures us of the reality and primacy of those eternal values which Christ came to reveal. This is the true Christianity, and we need not be discouraged about its prospects of victory if we look for them in the fruits of the spirit, and not in institutional statistics or successes of organization."

Was ever such a mass of verbiage! There is no rhyme or reason in it. Not one definite statement of doctrine, save that God is unchanging—followed by the necessity of change in our beliefs: therefore, of course, a change in our belief that God is unchanging. Strange rigmarole!

What are "the Eternal values that Christ came to reveal?" No answer! What is "sitting loose to tradition?" In what degree, where and how may traditions be a guide? No answer! What is that "experience" which, though an "experience," has no authority? No answer! What has he to say against a personal experience of the value of authority? No answer! What is "Christianity"? No answer! How does it carry on without institutions? No answer!

Yet it is from the pen of Dean Inge, a man whose whole public standing is that of one criticizing religious doctrine from the superior plane of our modern advance in knowledge, and that pen when it deals with any other matter than religion is as precise as any now writing and as clear.

I would not accuse such an intelligence as his from suffering the collapse of the "Modern Mind"—but he panders to it. He has an eye on the readers of his journalism.

\* \* \*

There stands the "Modern Mind," a morass.

The great difficulty of the intelligent in dealing with this thing, whether they be Catholic or skeptical, is the lack of hold. It is like fighting smoke. It affords a commentary on the famous tag that with stupidity the gods themselves will wrestle in vain.

What are you to do with a man who always argues in a circle? Who tells you that some political arrangement is good because it is "democratic," and when you ask  (a) whether it is as a fact democratic,  (b) why democracy is an evident good, answers you by saying that you are sinning against democracy and its holy name.

What are you to do with a man who does not recognize his own first principles? Who tells you that he believes a thing on the authority of a name or a bit of print, and who, when you ask him the grounds of his confidence in such, answers you by giving another name and another bit of print?

What are you to do with a man who uses the same word in different senses during the same discussion? As, for instance, who says he "believes in Evolution," meaning growth (which all men believe in), and in the same sentence make it mean: (a) The bestial origin of man's body—which is probable enough, (b) Darwin's theory of Mechanical Natural Selection, which is as dead as a door-nail.

What are you to do with a man who puts it forth as a foundation for debate that the human reason is no guide, and who then proceeds to reason through hundreds of pages on that basis?

Yet all that, and hundreds of derivatives therefrom, make up the horrible welter of the "Modern Mind."

Well, we must hope that intelligence will resume its rights, even against such; but the prospect is not cheerful. Meanwhile the monstrous apparition of the "Modern Mind" has produced one good among many evils; it has produced a belated Brotherhood of the Intelligent. We of the Faith and the cultured Pagans have a common opponent. A common donkey blocking the car, and needing to be shouldered off the lane into the ditch, breeds fellow-feeling between the Catholic and the clear-minded skeptic. Each feels a peculiar disgust with the "Modern Mind." So we have, at last, allies.

The "Modern Mind" feeds. The animal is nourished or it could not live. All moods must thus receive regular sustenance or perish. What is the food which aliments the "Modern Mind"? It absorbs two forms of nutrition—one from the imposed elementary school, one from the popular press. Between them they secure the continuity and permanence of the "Modern Mind." These two instruments were unknown to the past; they are of strong effect on the present. They are of effect throughout the whole of the modern European and American world, and their effect is increasing. I will state them in their order.

The first thing to be said about universal compulsory instruction as it is now arranged, is that it is necessarily at issue with the Catholic conception of society because it sets out upon a first principle which the Catholic conception of society denies. That is not a judgment agreeable to modern fashion, but it is true; and before we consider the particular way in which this institution sustains the "Modern Mind," we must appreciate how and why it necessarily clashes with that Faith to which the "Modern Mind" is now the principal obstacle.

This first principle upon which universal compulsory instruction is based is the idea that a certain minimum of instruction in a certain category of learning is the *first* essential to right living. Other things come after; but a knowledge of these, at least, is indispensable to man and society, and must therefore be imposed on all by force. This category includes letters, that is, reading and writing, elementary arithmetic, by which ordinary civic occupations are carried on, some very general knowledge of the past and of contemporary nations, their geography and character, the whole tinctured with the (today) inevitable religion of Nationalism and a vague general ethic, humanitarian and therefore (unwittingly) positivist.

These having been imposed upon every child of the community by force, whether the parents are willing or unwilling, its other activities, such as religion, seem subsidiary. They may or may not be engaged in, and whether they are engaged in or not is indifferent to society and therefore to the State.

The Catholic conception of human nature is actively at issue with this. According to it, the first, the most necessary thing, is the teaching of the children, affirmatively, as a divine truth necessary not only to the conduct of its own life, but also to that of all society, the doctrines and the particular, defined, morals of the Catholic Church.

In comparison with instruction in that one prime essential, nothing else counts. It is good to be able to read and write and cast up simple sums; it is better still to know something of the past of one's people, and to have a true idea of the world around one. But these are nothing compared with the Faith.

Here is the first point of conflict between the Church and her enemies in the matter of this new instrument which is beginning to be of such prodigious effect throughout our imperilled civilization. Next let it be noted that there is another issue perhaps even graver, and that is, the issue between the Family and the State and between the full multiple life of free will in action and the uniform restricted death-in-life of things done by constraint and on a mechanical model.

As between the Family and the State, Catholic doctrine is fixed. The family is the unit. The parent is the natural authority *(auctoritas auctoris)*. The State is secondary to the family, and *especially* in the matter of forming a child's character by education. Now here the State of today flatly contradicts Catholic doctrine. It says to the parent, "What you will for your child must yield to what *I* will. If our wills are coincident, well and good. If not, yours must suffer. I am master." At least, so the State speaks to the poorer parent; to the richer it is more polite.

Many Catholics are afraid to say so, but that is, in Catholic terms, abominably bad morals: the morals of tyranny.

The issue between free will and constraint is less direct—but it is very real. It is not without significance that the claim to interfere by force not only in the all-important character of early instruction, but in a score of other domestic things, has gone side by side with the spread of fatalism in the world and with the inhuman concept of unalterable mechanical laws. It is not insignificant that the Church in the rare places and times when She had power to do so, did not compel the mind. During all that intense intellectual life of the thirteenth century, instruction was by choice: *endowed*—so that the poorest could reach the highest inspiration, but at the choice of the individual or family will, to be taken or left.

Compulsory universal instruction, then, clashes with every canon of Catholic social ethics, even in its compulsion, even in its universality, but especially in its choice of what it calls essentials.

Although these things are so, one may hear from the "Modern Mind" a plea which it is so confused as to hold applicable. It advances this argument: "I do not say that the things imposed by force upon the mass of young minds are the most ultimately important. All I say is that they are what none will differ about and what all will agree to be necessary to life in society. As to other, perhaps more important, but debated things, I keep neutral." Yet it should be evident that *how* things are taught, even things which have no direct relation with religious teaching, makes all the difference to the effect of an education. The teaching as a whole must be Catholic or non-Catholic. You cannot make a school which shall not be the one or the other, any more than you can make a home which shall not be the one or the other.

It is one of the sure tests of stupidity in those who discuss this matter when they put forward the plea that religion cannot come into the teaching of arithmetic; the very same people would violently object to having their own children taught arithmetic by one of whose morals and outlook they disapproved.

But arithmetic is not the only thing taught. Some kind of morals must be taught. And here a violent issue arises, which is an issue between diverse *orders;* for the *order* in which you teach morals makes all the difference.

Are you going to teach children that the excessive consumption of liquor is the prime evil of human life? Are you going to teach them that consideration for others is the highest duty of man? Are you going to teach them that kindness to animals is among the highest of virtues?

No one denies that drunkenness is a bad thing, or that cruelty to animals is a bad thing, or that the service of one's neighbor is a good thing; but the point is, in what *order* are you going to teach them, what *relative* importance are you going to give them? Everything turns on that. With one set of proportions you produce one type of character, with another, another. In one order you have Catholic morals, in another Protestant, in another Pagan.

Truth lies in proportion. It is proportion which differentiates a caress from a blow, a sneer from a smile. It is the sequence and the relative weight of doctrines, not the bald statement, that makes the contrast between what damns and what saves. Let a child experience through the working day and through most days of the year that this or that is emphasized in its teaching, and what is so emphasized becomes, for it, and for all its life, the essential.

Apart from this consideration—which applies to *all* subjects— there is a multitude of subjects in which the effect of teaching makes for truth or falsehood according to religious atmosphere.

Take a single example from elementary geography. It relates to Holland, a country the origin of whose religious opinions was mentioned on an earlier page.

A little while ago the Dutch authorities protested against a textbook used in our English (Protestant) elementary schools describing Holland as a wholly Protestant country—with sundry other remarks upon the virtues which presumably follow from such a character. The remark that Holland is a country wholly Protestant, and that the whole point of Holland is its Protestant-ism, would seem so obvious to nine out of ten modern Englishmen that they must have marvelled at any protest being made: yet it is, of course, a completely false statement, and the false-hood is highly characteristic of the way in which a religious atmosphere affects teaching.

Holland is a country largely divided between the two religions; rather more than half its people are Protestant, rather less than half are Catholic. The whole point of the Dutch exam-ple to a man trained in true history is the way in which a State which was, in its origins, artificially created by a revolt against taxation, next strengthened by a violently anti-Catholic temper, maintained for generations by an exclusion of Catholics from power, has come now to something like a balance of the two cultures. Yet it is almost inevitable that such a textbook statement should be imposed upon our elementary schools, which have to accept what our official historians—brought up on stuff like Motley—themselves so naively believe.

There is a case taken from elementary geography. With his-tory, of course, the thing is patent. If you are teaching the official nationalist history of our day, you are teaching anti-Catholic his-tory, and there is no way out of it. The whole business from A to Z is anti-Catholic propaganda.

Now this instrument of universal compulsory education must obviously be of vast effect, but of *how* vast an effect it may be, what changes in society may be effected by the manipulation of it, people have hardly yet realized.

It originated in the French Revolution, and the first man to give form to *one* of its constituents was Danton, when he said that, after bread, the first need of the populace was instruction. The seed was sown. It was—to the reformers of the eighteenth century —a truism that all would be well with men if they had "light." Ignorance in terrestrial matters they thought the parent of all ill. Since this was so, to make elementary instruction, at least, in such matters, *universal,* seemed an unmixed good. But how could one ensure its being universal unless one made it compulsory?

Such was the chain of policy: the enormous result was not intended. The sole intention was to give citizens what the limited views of its authors thought an obvious advantage.

The idea was carried out in the course of the nineteenth century more or less thoroughly, according as the organizations of the various nations and the degree of their servility to the State made compulsion easier or harder to apply, and according to the degree in which opinion accepted this new doctrine that elementary instruction was all-important.

In England, with a population more and more urban as time went on, and more thoroughly controlled than any other by a very numerous and highly organized police, the system reached perfection. For a lifetime past hardly a family (below a certain high level of income) has escaped the huge machine. It has stamped its mold upon the whole nation and changed it profoundly.

But if this new force has been most thoroughly applied in England, it is almost as effective in other western countries, and is now the strongest political instrument of our time.

It is strange how long it took people to wake up to the situation. Even now the most of men have not begun to speculate on its possible use for certain definite ends of propaganda. But the great religious quarrel in France, the change worked by the elementary school in Britain, the recurrent agitations in the United States against public grants for the schools of a religious minority, have begun to make the latent power of the system apparent.

The wisest observers now clearly perceive that if compulsory elementary universal instruction be captured and used to a certain end, it can completely transform the character of all society. When we remember that the system is supported and confirmed by the ever-increasing network of public examinations, all taking the same history, geography and philosophy for granted, the formidable character of this new thing should be sufficiently apparent.

Therefore, the inevitable conflict between the Catholic and the non-Catholic conceptions of human nature, life and destiny, cannot but make the elementary school their battlefield.

There are those who think the problem can be solved by the compromise of tolerating the existence of Catholic schools, side by side with those of the common kind—schools with Catholic teachers and the right to teach Catholic doctrine at odd hours.

Such a subjection has never passed current in countries of Catholic culture; but in the Prussian Reich it has worked easily for a long lifetime, and in Britain for as long.

The only peril (it is claimed) lies in sundry individual anti-Catholic false statements in historical textbooks, or, in morals, specific assertions opposed to the Catholic Faith. Let the Catholic object to such and such particulars in the textbooks; if these are eliminated, all will be well.

It is not so. These Catholic tolerated schools are supported with State money as State institutions only so long as they conform to State standards of instruction, *and therefore to State doctrines in the thing taught.* No solution can be reached on such lines.

Such a compromise presupposes a common body of truth in morals, a common standard of philosophy, a common attitude towards the past, the external world and the nature of man. It presupposes this common attitude to be the one important thing, the foundation upon which the *less* important differences in beliefs and morals arise.

The presupposition is false. There is no such thing as a primal, neutral core of truth with various particular accretions around it of Catholic, Protestant, Jewish, or Mahommedan feeling. Any one philosophy strongly held permeates the whole body of ideas and actions, and, inevitably, if you have a single system of textbooks, of inspection and regulation, of examinations, and an official curriculum of teaching, all these will have one general philosophy running through them. The universal machine imposed upon all in the years when the character is formed, will imprint its own philosophy, both directly and still more by indirect influence. If you doubt this, look around you.

Such a philosophy may well be that of the majority, but can never be that of *all*. Any philosophy not of the machine must suffer, and in the case of so distinctive an entity as the Catholic Church—a thing distinct from all the rest of the world, understanding and penetrating, yet separate from the world—the hostile character of such a machine should be self-evident.

I am proposing no solution, I am making no prophecy; but I am stating an issue which none, I think, can, upon consideration, deny. The elementary school, mastered by the lay State, and imposing its instruction by compulsion, is of its nature hostile to the Faith, whether hostile intention be present or no.

How hostile we can see by observing that it has produced and continues to nourish the "Modern Mind."

But how has it done so? How is this novel and gigantic instrument of policy accountable for this particular disease? To answer that question consider the affinities between the two and the way in which they will naturally act and react the one on the other till each is cause and effect at once.

A universal and compulsory system of instruction has for its first and main effect *uniformity*. It produces to a pattern. It fills the millions of a nation (at the age when the mind is being fixed) with one set of ideas to the exclusion of others. No mere limited freedom of choice in textbooks and teachers can prevent this effect, when the whole system is subject to State regulation, supervision, examination and test. Indeed, it can be verified by experience that there is sometimes even more diversity of result in a centralized system of education than in one where local authorities and various religious bodies have power of selecting books and instructors. Thus in France it is a frequent complaint, on the part of those with a passion for national unity, that the elementary school does not provide it, while in England, where the system is theoretically far less rigid, no one can or does complain of stray differences in its results, for there are little or no differences apparent. It is not the particular form of the system,

it is its *universal* character which is of this effect. On reflection
we see that it must be so. A body of national teachers will come
into being and will be informed with a corporate spirit. They will
be trained all in much the same fashion to the same fixed "standards" and with the same ends in view. They will teach under
the shadow of a vast bureaucracy and to ends set them by an army
of inspectors, examiners and departmental officials.

You have, therefore, here one essential condition of the "Modern Mind"; its lack of diversity; its mechanical deadness. This,
when it is achieved, reacts in turn upon the elementary school,
and each, the agent and the object, the school and the scholar,
increases the sterility of the other. Uniformity acquired by the
second makes easier the action of the first, and both conform
to a common fixedness.

Indirectly but more strongly still this mechanical uniformity
tends to exclusion of ideas. That which is not taught at all to
a child, or is taught as something subsidiary, falls out of his
consciousness or is diminished therein. For the most part what
is not emphasized is not believed to exist. Often, from its
unfamiliarity, that which is a stranger to education in childhood,
is thought incredible by the grown man.[6]

Were there multiple, individual diversity as there was when
education was voluntary, men would be acquainted in early life
with its presence even when they did not experience it themselves. But, where all is the same, the very possibility of difference ceases to be accepted. Now the ideas excluded under our
system of universal compulsory State instruction are necessarily
those the absence of which produce the "Modern Mind" as
readily as the absence of certain elements in food scrofula.

Here is an example: the attitude of the "Modern Mind" to
illiteracy. The chief subjects of elementary instruction are reading and writing. Therefore a weakness or incapacity in these

---

6. See for instance with what difficulty the nineteenth century schoolboy,
   brought up on the official history of his time, could appreciate in manhood
   the idea that our exclusive patriotism was a modern thing! See how he read
   it, when he became a man, into the medieval history of his country!

two departments becomes the test of inferiority. One nation may build, sing, paint, fight, better than another; but if it has a larger proportion unable to read, it is branded as the lesser of the two. A Spaniard of Estremadura may carve stone images as living as those of the thirteenth century, but if he cannot read, the "Modern Mind" puts him far below the loafer picking out racing tips in his paper. In the same connection we all know how the restriction of writing to a comparatively small class in the past is put forward as an example of our progress. That writing was then an art, that its materials were expensive, that to draw up a letter in, say, the eleventh century needed as much special training and expense as it does today to engrave a brass tablet— all that is missed. The "Modern Mind" notes that there was less writing, and is satisfied that such a lack was inexcusable.

And here let us note in passing a practical effect of Universal Compulsory Instruction which is at first not logically apparent but the reason of which can be discovered; I mean its fostering of that illusion of "Progress" which is so intimate a part of the "Modern Mind." The elementary school does, in practice, make the less intelligent believe that they are better than their fathers and better off as well; materially in advance of them and morally in advance of them. It might be thought that this folly of vain glory was but an accident of our time. The stupid opinion of our time is all for "Progress" as an inevitable succession from worse to better—Wednesday better than Tuesday, and Tuesday, than Monday. This illusion, bred of Pride and Ignorance, appears (it may be said) in our official instruction, because it happens to be the fashion. Let the mood change, let some succession of catastrophes awaken in men a sense of decline, and vulgar opinion will renounce the illusion of Progress, will praise the past at the expense of the present, and the new mood will reflect itself in all institutions, including that of the educational bureau.

This is an error. Compulsory Universal Instruction will *always* make for the illusion of Progress, because it must justify itself by affirming improvement. It would stultify itself if it did not regard itself as a progressive good, and a proof of continued advance from a time in which it was unknown.

Universal Compulsory Instruction contains also on its *compulsory* side, as well as in the matter of its universality, a force making for the creation of the "Modern Mind." Compulsion, long continued, breeds acceptance; and the acceptance without question of such authority as it meets—especially that of print— "blind faith" we have said, "divorced from reason"—is a very mark of the "Modern Mind."

This atmosphere of compulsion pervades the whole affair. It is not the presence of compulsion affirmed in the laws (upon which Elementary State Instruction is based today) which counts here, it is the daily practice of it by millions—by all. The Parent does not choose his child's instructor nor the nature of his teaching, both are imposed by the Civil Authority. The child goes daily to and from that institution, has its whole life colored by it, knows that its attendance is not an order of its parents but a public command enforced by the Police.

All teaching is dogmatic. Dogma, indeed, means only "a thing taught," and teaching not dogmatic would cease to be teaching and would become discussion and doubt. But this new sort of teaching by force has an added effect, beyond that found in any other kind of teaching. It is at once teaching and law, and those subjected to it are inoculated from its earliest years with a paralysis in the faculty of *distinction*—of clarity in thought through analysis. Look around you and note the incapacity for strict argument, the impatience with exact definition, the aversion to controversy (mother of all truth) and the facility in mere affirmation. Herein lies their root.

---

The second great new instrument nourishing the "Modern Mind" is the popular Press. Here, happily, there is not such an issue as in the case of compulsory education.

In the field of compulsory education the issue is absolute and inevitable. A universal and homogeneous system of compulsory instruction imposed by the State upon the family cannot fit in with the Catholic Church. Even with a society homogeneously Catholic it could not fit, for automatically the Catholic spirit would dissolve its compulsory quality and its mechanical uniformity of universal action. The Catholic spirit automatically restores diversity of mind and freedom.

But with the Press it is otherwise. The popular Press is often represented as a solvent of religion, and in particular a solvent of Catholicism; but there is nothing in its nature to make it so.

It happens to have arisen in a world where the false conception that religion was a private affair had taken root. Therefore it does not spread the atmosphere of religion, it does not concern itself with life in the order which true religion demands. It presents as matters of chief importance things not even important in natural religion, let alone in the eyes of the Church.

It tends, for instance, to substitute notoriety for fame, and to base notoriety upon ridiculous accidents of wealth or adventure. Again, it presents as objects for admiration a bundle of things incongruous: a few of some moment, the great part trivial. Above all it grossly distorts.

Its chief force as a sustainer of the "Modern Mind" lies in its power to intensify any disease prevalent in the masses, and especially in the human dust of our great towns. Thus the "Modern Mind" dislikes thinking: the popular Press increases that sloth by providing sensational substitutes. Disliking thought, the "Modern Mind" dislikes close attention, and indeed any sustained effort; the popular Press increases the debility by an orgy of pictures and headlines. The "Modern Mind" ascribes a false authority to reiteration; the popular Press serves it with ceaseless iteration. The "Modern Mind" has accepted a mythology of the prehistoric and loves to hear both of marvels in connection with prehistory and of its own superiority to its remote ancestry: the popular Press crams it with food for such an appetite. It will give countless millions of years to a bit of bone of which no mortal knows the age; it will provide at call the most horrible beasts for our forbears, adding to them a peculiar vileness in morals to spice the dish—though beasts can do no wrong.

In all these ways and twenty others the popular Press as we have it today thrusts the "Modern Mind" lower than it would otherwise have fallen, swells its imbecility and confirms it in its incapacity for civilization and therefore for the Faith.

But the popular Press does not act thus from a sort of conspiracy against truth and religion and our high, inherited Catholic culture; it acts thus because the society in which and by which it lives has not yet recovered its religion; if, indeed, it shall ever do so. In a society restored to unity of religion and to devotion to it, the popular Press would recover and reflect that general mood.

There are, molding a popular newspaper, three forces: the advertisement subsidy by which it lives, the particular desires of its owner, and the appetite of the public for that particular sheet. Of these the third is much the most important. The first, advertisement revenue, is mainly dependent upon public demand for the paper. The effect of the proprietor lies chiefly in his power of private blackmail (especially, in parliamentary countries, of blackmail exercised against politicians) and in his power (when he acts in combination with his few fellows) to suppress a truth of public interest. But the owner of a widely read newspaper, even when, by some accident, he happens to be a man of intelligence, hardly ever imposes an idea.

It may be said with justice that a popular Press in our day will always tend to be demagogic, and therefore somewhat offensive in moral tone. In some countries, notably in England, it has submerged the old cultivated and educated press of a generation ago. It is, therefore, commonly ridiculous; but it does not follow that it is a negative force against the power of the Catholic Church in the modern world.

For all its vulgarity it may indirectly be of service to the Faith, for the discussion of religion today has a high interest value, and thus the popular Press has certain rough uses as an arena for that most profitable form of debate.

It would be hopeless, I think, to expect just now in any country the advent of a popular paper which should act, however indirectly, as an instrument for actually spreading the Faith. But I doubt whether the judgment should be passed that in any country the popular Press will, in the main, become an instrument *against* the spreading of the Faith: it will reflect, very roughly and coarsely, the main currents of popular opinion in this matter as in others.

It will, for instance, reflect the modern religion of Nationalism until that religion begins to wane. It will reflect the desire which the mob has always had for spectacles of wealth, violence and peril. It will exaggerate the popularity of what is popular and the unpopularity of what is unpopular.

In itself it is not our enemy, but, then, neither can it be used by us in favor of the truth, save in its character of an arena for debate. There it may in the future become (it has not yet so become) an instrument of real value.

The reason it has not yet become such is the still prevailing ignorance on the elements of theological discussion, coupled with the fatigue and decay of intelligence in a period where words have grown meaningless or contradictory (for instance, the word "Temperance") and have been turned into a kind of false currency to take the place of thought.

Meanwhile the novel power of the popular Press is having one curious effect, which is, I think, to be deplored, in connection with the situation of the Church in the modern world. It is this:

The specialization of Catholic journalism in all countries today, or nearly all countries (Ireland is largely an exception), excludes a Press secular in interest but Catholic in tone. Your widely read newspaper makes a point of what it regards as religious neutrality (aiming as it does at the largest possible circulation); therefore the Catholic writer can only put forth his arguments in publications which are *(a)* confined to specifically clerical activities, *(b)* read only by his co-religionists. They tell you much of the clergy; they discuss pilgrimages, centenaries, new ecclesiastical foundations; they have controversies upon individuals or doctrines when such are attacked. They do not reach the non-Catholic masses.

But of all that I will write when we come, at the close of this book, to consider our modern opportunities of recovery.

With this I end the analysis of those main forces of opposition which the Church has to meet at the moment, and turn to those interesting young strangers, the New Arrivals: they that are to be our main opponents of tomorrow.

# 5

## NEW ARRIVALS

While the Faith is engaged in its main modern battle with the positive forces of Nationalism and Anti-Clericalism, the negative force of intellectual decline, those who are to be our next antagonists, after these are spent, wait in reserve: they will conduct the attack in the near future.

To change the metaphor, the New Arrivals are waiting in the wings while the Main Opposition of our day still fills the stage and the Survivals are filing away to their exits.

Now to appreciate the character of the New Arrivals at any epoch of the Church's history is essential to understanding Her position at that epoch: but it is also the hardest task of all. It is essential, because, by the nature of the New Arrivals do we test the effect the Church is having on Her time: the reaction which She, for the moment, provokes. It is difficult because the things to be studied are not yet developed. They are still slight in substance or embryonic in form. The Survivals we know thoroughly. They are our acquaintances from childhood, our senior friends. Everyone recognizes them and knows all about them. They were familiars of our own parents and we half regret their passing. But the New Arrivals are oddities, disturbing or ignored. Many of us have hardly come across more than one of them. Such as we have met come little into our lives, and, when they do, so irritate us with their crudity or incomprehensibility that it is easier to turn aside from them and forget them.

The dear old "Higher Critic," the cousinly "Agnostic" with his test tubes and little geological hammer, these are of the Household as it were: furniture as domestic to us as the landscape of home. And Harnack still with us, Renan and Huxley lately gone, the decorous melancholy of Arnold, are on the best-used shelf of our library. But when it comes to the men who chat pleasantly with the dead, to the men who like discords in music, to the men who prefer the ugly in paint and stone, to the men who openly despair, to the men who willingly share their wives, to the men who laud what we used to call perversion in sex, to the men who find honor quaint and to the men who respect theft and swindling, we not only feel out of place but superior and impatient, as though these barbaric futilities were so ephemeral as hardly to be taken seriously. But we should beware of that mood or it may make us underestimate our enemies.

When I say "we," I speak of my own generation, and I that am writing here am close on sixty; it may be that men and women in the thirties would write differently and feel for the New Arrivals more respect.

Well, when we do look long enough at the New Arrivals pressing to come forward, we discover one very interesting mark common to them all: they are at issue with the Catholic Church not directly on doctrine as were their elders, but on *morals.* Morals derive from doctrine, of course, and indirectly the quarrel is doctrinal: as all human conflicts are. But the distinctive note of the New Arrivals is that they do not propose new theses to be held in theology, as did the heresiarchs of old, nor first principles in philosophy which contradict the first principles of the Faith, as did our nineteenth century opponents, but that they have a new ethic—or perhaps none.

All the Survivals and even the agents of the present Main Opposition maintained and maintain in practice (and more or less even in theory) the bulk of Catholic morals. They inherited these from the past. They were and are part of that general European civilization which was the creation of the Catholic Church. But the New Arrivals are, in greater and lesser degree, shedding so much of this heritage that they are of a novel kind: they speak in a new language.

Herein lie both the peril and the acute interest of our moment.

We are approaching unknown forms in the conflict between the Church and the world. We are about to meet—or our children are—not the assault of rebels, men of our own speech and manner, but the assault of aliens. Hitherto it has been Civil War: it is soon to be Invasion.

Hitherto the mysteries have been abandoned as unreasonable or illusory; for instance, the Eucharist, the Incarnation. The strict discipline of the Faith has been rejected as too harsh or too meticulous: Theology has been ridiculed as a map of *Terra Incognita,* a whimsical imagination. The official framework of the Church has been attacked as tyrannical and man-made, lacking true authority: the main doctrines—even of the Godhead—as lacking evidence and therefore negligible. Hitherto all manner of competing systems in thought have been proposed for the supplanting of the Faith. But throughout these age-long quarrels the tradition of Catholic culture has been preserved. Those in theory most opposed to the Faith have in practice followed the conventions of Europe. Even when they attacked property or marriage it was in the name of Justice. They maintained the concept of human dignity. They were indignant, in all their vagaries, against evils (such as oppression of the poor) which the Faith itself had taught men to hate. *Now* something quite other is beginning to show. A strange New Paganism. We are concerned to discover its quality, what older allies it will find and whether it may not be the forerunner of some new positive religion.

What quality has it, this New Paganism? To what allies older than itself may it rally? Does it portend the advent of a new positive religion to be set up against the Church in the last days?

Those three questions I would now examine:

## Neo-Paganism

It is the common and very true remark of those who survey the modern world as a whole, and especially of those who survey it from the central standpoint, which is that of the Church, and more particularly of those who survey it from the heart of contemporary discussion, which is in France, that the struggle now lies between the Catholic Church and Paganism.

That is now a truism to all save the provincial and belated. But *what* Paganism? Therein lies our interest. Certainly it is not the Paganism of that radiant Greco-Latin antiquity from which we sprang. The pristine things are not recovered through decay. Senility may be called second childhood, but we do not find in it the eagerness and vitality of youth. Popular faith having rotted into that base welter called the "Modern Mind," there has arisen a growth from the slime. That growth is certainly *a* Paganism. But a Paganism of what character? Of what smell, taste and stuff? We must know that if we are to guess at its results.

First, why do we call it a Paganism at all?

Paganism at large may be defined as natural religion acting upon man uncorrected by revelation.

If the word "uncorrected" seems unsuitable—for after all, natural religion is true as far as it goes, and the truth does not, *quâ* truth, need correction—let me substitute for the term "uncorrected" the term "unsupplemented." Paganism is what the special language of St. Paul calls "the old Adam," and what we today would put in terms more normal to our idiom as "the natural man."

Let us see in what this religious attitude (for it is a religious attitude—as are indeed all fundamental attitudes of the mind) consists.

Man has a conscience; he knows the difference between right and wrong. He also is necessarily aware of certain great problems upon his nature, end, and destiny which he may not be able to solve, but the solution of which, *if it could be reached,* must be far more important for him than anything else. Does he only mature, grow old and die, or is that process but part of a larger destiny? Have his actions permanent or only ephemeral consequences to himself? Are awful unseen powers to which he devotes gratitude, worship and fear, imaginations of his or real? Are his dead no longer in being? Is he responsible to a final Judge?

He may decide that as there is no evidence no conclusion is possible, that the search for it is a waste of effort and any apparent discovery thereof an illusion. But he cannot deny that on what the answer is—did he but know it—all conduct and all values turn.

He has a sense of beauty which is, in the average man, strongly founded, and consonant to the great Catholic doctrine that the Creation is good. He is necessarily informed by a sense of justice, and feels that some degree of conformity to it is necessary to the very existence of civil society. He recognizes (does the natural man inspired by natural religion) the folly and danger of excessive pride, of excessive appetite, anger, and the rest: for he has humor to keep him sane.

It might seem at first sight that man thus turned loose and sufficient unto himself would fall into a vague but contented philosophy under which we would live well balanced, as the animals live normally to their instincts, and that the Pagan would be the least troubled of men.

That man would so live if he were left free from the trammels of what calls itself "revelation" is the fundamental doctrine of all that movement which has been leading us back towards Paganism. There is already present among us the conception that Paganism, once re-established, will result in a decently happy world, at any rate a world happier than that world of Christendom which was formed throughout the centuries under the spell of the Faith.

But it is not so. There appears one eccentric point of supreme moment, most revealing, bidding us all pause. It is this: Paganism despairs. Man turned loose finds himself an exile. He grows desperate, and his desperation breeds monstrous things.

Each kind of Paganism came to suffer from horrid gods of its own at last, and these give to each Paganism its particular savor. But the mark of the New Paganism is that it has not reached these last stages by a long process of debasement. It is not entering a period of fresh life. Its gods are already the vile gods of complexity and weakness. The New Paganism is born precocious and diseased.

We conceive of the Pagan, when first we hear of his advent, as a normal man. We all sympathize with him in our hearts; we all understand him: many of us have been at one time or another (mostly in youth) of his company. What quarrel, we then asked, has revealed religion with him? Wherein lies his weakness? We know now. It lies in his rejection of a central spiritual truth, to wit, that man is permanently degraded in his own eyes—without escape: that he has in him the memory of things lost: that he is of heavenly stuff, condemned and broken. It is the doctrine which we Catholics call the Fall of Man.

We cannot use that doctrine as an argument against the Pagan, because if we do so we are, in the eyes of the Pagan, begging the question. But what will appeal to him and to any observer from without, is this: that Paganism, the natural man, acting without revelation, does *not* conform to his own nature: he is *not* in equilibrium and repose. It looks as though he ought to be, but in fact he is not. Before the advent of the Faith, even despair could struggle to be noble. But since the medicine for despair has been known, those who refuse the remedy turn base. Europe expecting it knew not what, was one thing. Europe baptized and apostatizing is quite another. Its material has changed.

The New Pagan, of course, laughs at the strict doctrine of the Fall; but he cannot laugh at the actual fact that man, when he acts as though he were sufficient to himself, not only permanently, necessarily and regularly does a myriad things of which he is himself ashamed, not only lacks the power to establish his imaginary healthy normal condition, but increasingly, as his Pagan society progresses, falls into worse and worse evils.

That is patently true. It is not a theory of what *should* happen when men cease to accept the truth upon man's nature: it is a statement of what *does* actually happen, witnessed to by all contemporary history and by the experience of individual characters. The old pre-Catholic Paganism did evil but admitted it to be evil. One of the greatest, and, I think, the most tragic lines in Latin verse is that famous phrase:

*Video meliora, proboque: deteriora sequor.*

It is a very epitome of the human story: of one man and of all.

But the New Paganism works in an attempted denial of good and evil which degrades all it touches.

Well, then, we say "Pagan society ends in despair." But

despair is not normal to men; despair is not the healthy mental state of the healthy natural creature. To say that it is so would be a contradiction in terms. Therefore do we find the old Paganism of the classics accompanied by a perpetual attempt to cheat despair by the opiates of beauty or of stoic courage.

But the New Paganism lives in despair as an atmosphere to be breathed, lives on it as a food by which to be nourished.

The New Paganism then, which is just raising its head, has this quality distinguishing it from the old: that it is beginning where the old left off.

If all Paganisms end in despair, ours is accepting it as a foundation. *That* is the special mark we have been seeking to distinguish this New Arrival. Hence the lack of reason which is intellectual despair, the hideous architecture and painting and writing which are aesthetic despair, the dissolution of morals which is ethical despair.

The thing is as yet unformed and only shocking in isolated instances. It is tentative as yet, not universal: rather appearing, so far, as a series of special lapses from the old Christian standards of civilization in this, that and the other respect, than as a mode. Some few deliberately detestable buildings and sculptures in our towns, (especially in our capitals): books, still somewhat eccentric, portraying every vice; the forced and still novel apology in speech for evil of every kind—preferably for the worst: all these are still no more than isolated insults and challenges. The New Paganism is still no more than a New Arrival. But it is rapidly growing; it is also gathering cohesion; and it cannot but appear in full and formidable strength within a comparatively short period as historical time is reckoned.

We elder people may not live to see the thing full blown, though I think we shall—noting as I do the pace at which change is proceeding; but our children will certainly see it. *When it is mature we shall have, not the present isolated, self-conscious insults to beauty and right living, but a positive coordination and organized affirmation of the repulsive and the vile.*

The New Paganism is advancing to its completion. It is about to take on body and to act as *one*.

To appreciate that truth take the instance of Marriage. Antique Paganism held the institution of marriage, but of marriage as a civil contract and dissoluble. When the Catholic Church had succeeded to the Pagan Empire it declared marriage *holy* and *indissoluble.* It affirmed of marriage and the instincts on which marriage was based, not only that they were good but that the institution itself was a Sacrament.

The Manichaean—that is, the Puritan—regarded these instincts as evil. The Church restricted them outside the sphere of marriage; The Manichaean condemned them altogether. The Neo-Pagan objects to both. He would set up man as an animal. He would, so far, make of marriage nothing but a civil contract terminable on the consent of both parties; soon he must make it terminable at the will of only one. The older heretics in this matter emphasized the human misery caused by the doctrine of indissoluble marriage, denied its divine sanction and worked to abolish its consequences in law. The New Pagans reject it from the root. Logically the Neo-Pagan should get rid of the institution of marriage altogether; but the very nature of human society, which is built up of cells each of which is a family, and the very nature of human generation, forbid such an extreme. Children must be brought up and acknowledged and sheltered, and the very nature of human affection, whereby there is the bond of affection between the parent and the child, and the child is not of one parent but of both, will compel the Neo-Pagan to modify what might be his logical conclusion of free love and to support some simulacrum of the institution of marriage. But his aim is opposed to the whole scheme, and we may truly say that the facility and frequency of divorce is the test of how far any society once Christian has proceeded towards Paganism.

Neo-Paganism grows prodigiously. The process has till recently been masked by the fragmentary survival of the Catholic Scheme, in attenuated and rapidly disappearing forms, throughout the Protestant culture; the tradition of free Will for instance, with its strong effects upon the organization of society, still lingers, retarding the return of servile conditions in Industrial England. You may even note with surprise occasional spasmodic rebellions by the individual against monopoly, legal, economic, or political: the survival, however vague and attenuated, of some dogma such as that of future reward and punishment for conduct in this life, or of human equality in despite of riches.

These remnants of Catholic doctrine both put a brake upon the pace of the great change and hide the process from the eyes of the average observer. But I do not see what chance of survival these fragments have in the modern world outside the Catholic body itself: the full *corpus* of Catholic faith and discipline in communion with Rome.

So long as there were definite Protestant creeds, more or less thought out and sustained by logic of a kind, so long as men could say *why* they thought and acted thus and thus, Paganism was kept out.

Whether this were to the advantage or disadvantage of mankind may be debated; just as one may debate whether it is better for a body to be warped or to be dead; but at any rate, so far as our present problem goes, these poor survivals of isolated and (in large part) distorted Catholic doctrines, oppose the return of Paganism.

Take, for instance, the Catholic doctrine of Charity. Out of that sprang, in the Middle Ages, and has been carried on to our own time, the whole body of social services, relief of the poor, hospitals, and the rest. These continue after a fashion, though the tradition outside the Catholic body has degenerated into sentimentalism on the one side and wild egalitarian extravagance upon the other. But present as are for the moment these distortions of sane Catholic truth, they cannot survive, because they do not answer the question "Why?" Why should one be charitable to one's fellow men? Why should one be at a burden, social or personal, of tending the sick with particular care and saving suffering, even to the poorest?

The old Paganism did not do these things. It permitted, for sport, such cruelty to man as Catholicism alone dispelled.

Most people, if they were asked to answer this question "Why?" would reply that such Charity was part of men's natural instincts; but all Pagan history and Pagan literature is there to prove the contrary; or at any rate, that if a certain measure of Charity be part of natural religion, and thus admitted by Pagan man, he does not act upon it. For, when a consistent creed is absent, the various parts of moral action are disassociated one from another, and all rapidly fail.

To take another instance. Why should I believe in moral sanctions applicable in a future life? So long as people went definitely by an accepted body of doctrine, such as the Calvinist, even so long as they accepted the authority of canonical scripture (though at their own individual interpretation) there was cohesion and therefore a principle of survival in the whole of what they thought and did. But when these creeds and authorities have gone—and take the white world as a whole, there is not much of them left today outside the Catholic Church—no guide to conduct remains but the instincts of men left to themselves, uncorrected, and the tendency to satisfy those instincts, even to their own hurt.

Paganism once erected into a system, once having taken on full shape, and proceeding to positive action, must necessarily become a formidable and increasingly direct opponent of the Catholic Church. The two cannot live together, for the points upon which they would agree are not the points which either thinks essential.

The clash must arise at first indirectly. A Pagan state makes certain laws which are repugnant to the Catholic conscience, laws concerning marriage or property, or domestic habits in eating and drinking, or concerning the freedom of labor, or any other function of the dignity of man. It proposes, let us say, what is called the "sterilization of the unfit," or compulsion in the matter of hours and wages ("compulsory arbitration"—the beginning of fully servile institutions)—or "eugenics," or the compulsory limitation of progeny, or any other nastiness.

In no such examples—and one might add a hundred more— would it be possible for the Catholic individual or the Catholic body to approve or even to stand aside as a neutral.

We have seen how this is so in the case of a universal compulsory educational system—there the Catholic objection is obvious. But it is present also, though less obvious, in any other hypothetical case you may consider. There will arise as the New Paganism spreads instances in which a Catholic finds himself asked to obey a law which he cannot in conscience obey—as, for instance, to make a declaration of mental incapacity in a dependent, well-knowing that this will legally involve castration. There cannot be an indefinite postponement of the issue.

I have suggested that the threat of Paganism returning among the white races, and the strength of Paganism when it shall have returned, will be presumably enhanced by a sort of moral alliance between it and the exterior Paganism of the East, of Asia; and not only of Asia, but, for that matter, of Africa too.

Now such a statement sounds, when it is put thus simply and shortly, and today, too unlikely to be acceptable. Its unlikeliness is even violent in the ears of the modern man. We have stood apart for centuries from organized Heathendom: that great sea surrounding the island of Christendom.

Latterly—that is, during the last three centuries, but especially during the nineteenth—we had even grown to despise the heathen world. It was far weaker than ourselves in military power, and in nearly all those arts of life which, even as we lost our own religion, we had come to regard as the most important.

But great tendencies are not to be judged by contemporary experience alone; still less by an inherited habit of thought from the past. We have to strike a curve and to find out the future probable development of that curve. It is worthless merely to strike a tangent from the particular moment in which we live. If you had hazarded such guesses, even as little as fifty years ago, as (1) that by 1929 the United States would be under prohibition, (2) that women would be sitting in the English House of Commons, (3) that Russia would be organized as an experiment in Communism under a clique of Jews, the suggestions would have sounded mad. Yet all these things have come to pass; and an observer of general tendencies in the course of the nineteenth century might have observed the beginnings of the forces which were to lead to such widespread changes.

What forces are present today making for a moral alliance

between the rising Paganism of the white man and the age-long Paganism of the black, brown and yellow man?

They are two, and they are sufficiently remarkable.

There is, in the first place, the sympathy between any one Paganism and another; for all forms of Paganism have in common the principle that man is sufficient to himself, and all have in common the negation of an absolute Divine Authority acting through revelation. They also have all in common the indulgence of human passion, and the practical permission of excess in it, whether in the passions of the appetite, or of anger, or of any other driving power in natural man.

In the second place there is propinquity. We are today mixed up with the old outer world as the classic Paganism of our forefathers never was. The Paganism of the Mediterranean basin, from which all our culture springs, was not originally affected very much by the Paganisms of Asia; by the Paganism of the Black races it was affected hardly at all: not because they would not have had some natural affinity with any other Paganism, but because there was little physical contact between them. Today such opportunity is universal, and is increasing in effect. Today the barrier, the only effective barrier, against such infiltration of Pagan ideas from races other than our own, is a strong anti-Pagan moral system and creed—and there is none such outside the Catholic Church.

If anyone doubt the menace of which I speak, let him note the nature of the degradation which has already, so recently and rapidly, come over our art. It is not the most important side of the affair, but it is the most easily discoverable, and therefore I mention it before the others. Thus, in our popular music the thing is glaring. The modern revolution in that art is a direct introduction of a force deriving from African Paganism. There is a strong though indirect and veiled corresponding influence in architecture, coming, not indeed from Africa, where Paganism was too debased to have any architecture at all, but from the same spiritual roots as nourished the monstrous moles of the ancient East. In this perversion the Prussians have been pioneers, the Bavarians after them, and the French are now following suit. England, happily for herself, lags behind. In Italy, with its strong Catholic culture, there is now a powerful reaction towards the ancestral beauty of European things as towards order in all its forms. But take Europe as a whole, and it is suffering heavily, and perhaps increasingly, in its external forms of art, not only architectural but pictorial, from the Pagan influence of Asia. In sculpture this repulsive innovation is notorious.

But by far the most profound effect of what I will call "The Pagan Alliance" appears in what lies at the root of everything—to wit, Philosophy.

Whether it be in the form of religious error, or in the commoner form of negation (which is the essential of the Buddhist business—what it is plainer to call, in Christian terms, Atheism), the influence of these ancient alien Paganisms is upon us everywhere.

At the same time we are growing more and more to respect the cultures arisen from those exterior paganisms. Our modern Neo-Pagans of European stock have welcomed this fraternization as a good thing. This welcome springs in part from their "brotherhood of the world" business; but much more is it a response of like to like.

It is not a good thing: it is a very bad thing, is this new respect for the non-Christian and anti-Christian cultures outside Europe. Insofar as it progresses it will inevitably breed, as it has already bred in so many, a contempt of Christian tradition and philosophy, as being things at once old-fashioned and puerile. There is more than one prominent European writer professing not only close acquaintance with, but reverence for, the Buddhist negation of God and of personal immortality: at the other extreme you have the respect for the Pagan ruthlessness and the Pagan doctrine of right-by-conquest.

There is no doubt that a powerful accelerator to this tendency was the sudden modern development of Japan. When the Japanese army defeated the Russian twenty odd years ago, it was a turning point in the history of our culture. When the Government of Great Britain took the step of allying itself openly with this new force—a policy which preceded that victory—it was a moral turning-point even more serious.

The thing has not yet gone so far as to become an immediate menace. The inter-communion between the new Paganism of Europeans and the very ancient Paganism of other races is as yet only faintly sketched out; but it is advancing. I cannot but believe that in another generation it will be powerful, apparent to all.

There remains, apart from the old Paganism of Asia and Africa, another indirect supporter of Neo-Paganism: a supporter which indeed hates all Paganism but hates the Catholic Church much more: a factor of whose now increasing importance the masses of Europe are not as yet aware: I mean the Mahommedan religion: Islam.

Islam presents a totally different problem from that attached to any other religious body opposed to Catholicism. To understand it we must appreciate its origins, character and recent fate. Only then can we further appreciate its possible or probable future relations with enemies of the Catholic effort throughout the world.

How did Islam arise?

It was not, as our popular historical textbooks would have it, a "new religion." It was a direct derivative from the Catholic Church. It was essentially, in its origin, a heresy: like Arianism or Albigensians.

When the man who produced it (and it is more the creation of one man than any other false religion we know) was young, the whole of the world which he knew, the world speaking Greek in the Eastern half and Latin in the Western (the only civilized world with which he and his people had come in contact) was Catholic. It was still, though in process of transformation, the Christian Roman Empire, stretching from the English Channel to the borders of his own desert.

The Arabs of whom he came and among whom he lived were Pagan; but such higher religious influence as could touch them, and as they came in contact with through commerce and raiding, was Catholic—with a certain admixture of Jewish communities.

Catholicism had thus distinctly affected these few Pagans living upon the fringes of the Empire.

Now what Mahomet did was this. He took over the principal doctrines of the Catholic Church—one personal God, Creator of all things; the immortality of the soul; an eternity of misery or blessedness—and no small part of Christian morals as well. All that was the atmosphere of the only civilization which had influence upon him or his. But at the same time he attempted an extreme *simplification*.

Many another heresiarch has done this, throwing overboard such and such too profound doctrines, and appealing to the less intelligent by getting rid of mysteries through a crude denial of them. But Mahomet simplified much more than did, say, Pelagius or even Arius. He turned Our Lord into a mere prophet, though the greatest of the prophets; Our Lady (whom he greatly revered, and whom his followers still revere), he turned into no more than the mother of so great a prophet; he cut out the Eucharist altogether, and what was most difficult to follow in the matter of the Resurrection. He abolished all idea of priesthood: most important of all, he declared for social equality among all those who should be "true believers" after his fashion.

With the energy of his personality behind that highly simplified, burning enthusiasm, he first inflamed his own few desert folk, and they in turn proceeded to impose their new enthusiasm very rapidly over vast areas of what had been until then a Catholic civilization; and their chief allies in this sweeping revolution were politically the doctrine of *equality,* and spiritually the doctrine of *simplicity.* Everybody troubled by the mysteries of Catholicism tended to join them; so did every slave or debtor who was oppressed by the complexity of a higher civilization.

The new enthusiasm charged under arms over about half of the Catholic world. There was a moment after it had started out on its conquest when it looked as though it was going to transform and degrade *all* our Christian culture. But our civilization was saved at last, though half the Mediterranean was lost.

For centuries the struggle between Islam and the Catholic

Church continued. It had varying fortunes, but for something like a thousand years the issue still remained doubtful. It was not till nearly the year 1700 (the great conquests of Islam having begun long before 700) that Christian culture seemed—for a time—to be definitely the master.

During the eighteenth and nineteenth centuries the Mahommedan world fell under a kind of palsy. It could not catch up with our rapidly advancing physical science. Its shipping and armament and all means of communication and administration went backwards while ours advanced. At last, by the end of the nineteenth century, more than nine-tenths of the Mahommedan population of the world, from India and the Pacific to the Atlantic, had fallen under the Government of nominally Christian nations, especially of England and France.

On this account our generation came to think of Islam as something naturally subject to ourselves. We no longer regarded it as a rival to our own culture, we thought of its religion as a sort of fossilized thing about which we need not trouble.

That was almost certainly a mistake. We shall almost certainly have to reckon with Islam in the near future. Perhaps if we lose our Faith it will rise.

For after this subjugation of the Islamic culture by the nominally Christian had already been achieved, the political conquerors of that culture began to notice two disquieting features about it. The first was that its spiritual foundation proved immovable; the second that its area of occupation did not recede, but on the contrary slowly expanded.

Islam would not look at any Christian missionary effort. The so-called Christian Governments, in contact with it, it spiritually despised. The ardent and sincere Christian missionaries were received usually with courtesy, sometimes with fierce attack, but were never allowed to affect Islam. I think it true to say that Islam is the only spiritual force on earth which Catholicism has found an impregnable fortress. Its votaries are the one religious body conversions from which are insignificant.

This granite permanence is a most striking thing, and worthy of serious consideration by all those who meditate upon the spiritual, and, consequently, the social, future of the world.

And what is true of the spiritual side of Islam is true of the geographical. Mahommedan rulers have had to give up Christian provinces formerly under their control: especially in the Balkans. But the area of Mahommedan *practice* has not shrunk. All that wide belt from the islands of the Pacific to Morocco, and from Central Asia to the Sahara desert—and south of it—not only remains intact but slightly expands. Islam is appreciably spreading its influence further and further into tropical Africa.

Now that state of affairs creates a very important subject of study for those who interest themselves in the future of religious influence upon mankind. The political control of Islam by Europe cannot continue indefinitely: it is already shaken. Meanwhile the spiritual independence of Islam (upon which everything depends) is as strong as, or stronger than, ever.

What affinities or support does this threat of Islam promise to the new enemies of Catholic tradition?

It will sound even more fantastic to suggest that Islam should have effect here than to suggest that Asiatic Paganism should. Even those who are directly in contact with the great Mahommedan civilization and who are impressed, as all such must be, by its strength and apparently invincible resistance to conversion, do not yet conceive of its having any direct effect upon Christendom. There are a few indeed who have envisaged something of the kind. But what they had to say was said before the Great War, was confined to individuals either isolated or eccentric, and produced no lasting impression upon either the French or the English: the only two European countries closely connected, as governing powers, with the Mahommedan. To the New World the problem is quite unfamiliar. It touches Mahommedanism nowhere save very slightly in the Philippines.

Nevertheless I will maintain that this very powerful, distorted simplification of Catholic doctrine (for that is what Mahommedanism is) may be of high effect in the near future upon Christendom; and that, acting as a competitive religion, it is not to be despised.

No considerable number of conversions to Mahommedanism

from Christendom is probable. I do not say that such a movement would not be possible, for anything is possible in the near
future, seeing the welter into which Christian civilization has
fallen. But I think it improbable, and even highly improbable,
because Mahommedanism advances in herd or mob fashion. It
does not proceed, as the Catholic religion does, by individual
conversions, but by colonization and group movement.

But there are other effects which a great anti-Catholic force
and the culture based upon it can have upon anti-Catholic forces
within our own boundaries.

In the first place it can act by example. To every man attempt-
ing to defend the old Christian culture by prophesying disaster
if its main tenets be abandoned, Mahommedanism can be
presented as a practical answer.

"You say that monogamy is necessary to happy human life,
and that the practice of polygamy, or of divorce (which is but
a modified form of polygamy) is fatal to the State? You are
proved wrong by the example of Mahommedanism."

Or again "You say that without priests and without sacraments
and without all the apparatus of your religion, down to the use
of visible images, religion may not survive? Islam is there to
give you the lie. Its religion is intense, its spiritual life permanent. Yet it has constantly repudiated all these things. It is violently anti-sacramental; it has no priesthood; it wages fierce war
on all symbols in the use of worship."

This example may, in the near future, be of great effect.
Remember that our Christian civilization is in peril of complete
breakdown. An enemy would say that it was living upon its past;
and certainly those who steadfastly hold its ancient Catholic doctrines stand today on guard as it were, in a state of siege; they
are a minority both in power and in numbers. Upon such a state
of affairs a steadfast, permanent, convinced, simple philosophy
and rule of life, intensely adhered to, and close at hand, may,
now that the various sections of the world are so much inter-
penetrating one and the other, be of effect.

The effect may ultimately be enhanced in the near future by
a political change.

We must remember that the subjection of the Mahommedan—a purely political subjection—was accomplished by nothing more subtle or enduring than a superiority in weapons and mechanical invention. We must further remember that this superiority dates from a very short time ago.

Old people with whom I have myself spoken as a child could remember the time when the Algerian pirates were seen in the Mediterranean and were still in danger along its southern shores. In my own youth the decaying power of Islam (for it was still decaying) in the Near East was a strong menace to the peace of Europe. Those old people of whom I speak had grandparents in whose times Islam was still able to menace the West. The Turks besieged Vienna and nearly took it, less than a century before the American Declaration of Independence. Islam was then our superior, especially in military art. There is no reason why its recent inferiority in mechanical construction, whether military or civilian, should continue indefinitely. Even a slight accession of material power would make the further control of Islam by an alien culture difficult. A little more and there will cease that which our time has taken for granted, the physical domination of Islam by the disintegrated Christendom we know.

---

That the New Arrival called Neo-Paganism will increase seems assured. That it will find support, positive from the older Paganism, negative from Islam as a fellow opponent of Catholicism, is possible or probable—though the modes of such support are not apparent today. But will it long remain as the Main Opposition when it shall have come to maturity? Or will it give way to some New Religion, with definite tenets and an organization of its own? Is there any appearance as yet of such a development? That is what we may next examine, and we must begin by looking at one or two typical bodies of the sort already in existence in order to decide whether they threaten to grow, or point to what might succeed them.

Outside the Catholic Church, we say, what was once Christendom is rapidly becoming Pagan: Pagan after a new fashion, but still Pagan. It is falling into the mood that man is sufficient to himself, and all the consequences of that mood will follow under a general color of despair.

But will this mood, after a first trial, be supplanted by a new religion sufficiently universal, organized and strong to challenge the Catholic Church? At present there is no sign of such a thing. None is present among the New Arrivals. But may not some such force soon arise?

It is very probable. It is not certain.

It is probable, because man can with difficulty persist in mere ideas or abstractions. He can with difficulty live on such thin food. He needs the meat of doctrine defined, of a moral code also defined—and with instances. He needs the institutions of a ritual and of all the external framework of worship. Moreover, man corporate demands answers to the great questions which face him: the problems of his own origin, nature and destiny. Man as an individual can decide them to be insoluble and lead his life—not easily—under the burden of that decision. But man in society does not repose in such negations. Therefore is the production of a new positive religion (with a special character of its own, a ritual, a doctrine) probable.

But it is not *certain,* for we know that, as a fact, great societies have long persisted content with a social scheme in which conventions take the place of doctrine and in which no defined philosophy clothed with external ritual and supported by organization is universal or even common. And when we consider the present situation we do not discover anything (as yet) from which, as from a seed, this new religion could spring.

It would seem, to begin with, that there will be no resurrection of the Protestant sects.

Not so long ago these were actual religions, and in particular Calvinism, with its fierce logic, iron conviction and completeness of structure, all informed with the French character of its creator. More loosely defined, but, still, organized and individual, heretical or schismatical bodies existed side by side with Calvinism. One could discover in each of these an ethic of its own, and, for all the Protestant ones combined, a fairly defined Protestant ethic or tone of mind. Meanwhile the Greek Church nourished an antagonism rather political than doctrinal and was also a powerful adverse force. But today these forces seem to have passed beyond the possibility of resurrection. Even the political strength of the Greek Church has been put out of action permanently by the effects of the Great War and revolution, with a gang of international adventurers replacing the old power of the Czardom and presiding over the ruin they have made.

I do not mean to deny that the strong evangelical spirit of Protestantism, and particularly of Calvinism, does not survive and is not an opponent; but when one is speaking of its resurrection as a *religion* for the future one must consider doctrine; and its doctrine has so thoroughly dissolved in the last fifty years that its re-establishment is hardly conceivable.

It is debatable, as I have said, whether this change is one for the worse or the better: on that point we may delay for a moment.

In one sense the power to hold any transcendental doctrine shows the soul to be still awake and therefore capable of achieving true transcendental doctrine, while those who lose the sense of the supernatural will be more difficult of approach.

On the other hand, with the loss of doctrine has gone the loss of support and framework of what opposed us. For instance, a Calvinist of the old school, with his passionately held dogma of salvation by faith, had for the ornament and ritual of the Catholic Church a correspondingly fierce hatred. His son today feels for such things indifference at the best or contempt at the worst; sometimes even admiration of adventitious beauty in Catholic rite and image.

At any rate whether this great change, the decay of the old Protestant bodies, be good or evil, it is an undoubted historical fact of our day. In Britain, as in Germany and the United States, the old catechisms, and what were in their odd way quasi creeds, have disappeared and we shall surely not hear of them again.

Where else may the seed of a New Religion, which shall grow to be the future arch-enemy of the Catholic Church, be sought?

We are surrounded by many novel experiments in worship and doctrine, but in none of them, not even in the Spiritualist, which would seem the strongest in structure, does there appear a vitality sufficient to produce any universal growth.

We find no such vitality in what may be called the "experiments in subjectivism."

Their name is legion. Half-a-dozen have cropped up within the later part of my own lifetime, and no doubt another dozen or more will crop up within the same length of time in the immediate future. It was only the other day that I came across the Sect of Deep-Breathers. In a sense the petty experiments thus based on what is called "subjectivism" are always with us, because almost any statement of religious experience through the individual, and that experience treated as a full authority without reference to the Church or any other form of authority, is subjectivism. Every revivalist meeting is an example of subjectivism. So is every book claiming to discover the truth through personal emotion.

But the subjective sects of this sort are swarming today with an especial vigor that merits attention if we are seeking for the possible signs of a new religion. At least, they are swarming in the English-speaking world.

There is no space to discuss the origins of these things; it must be sufficient to mention them. All ultimately derive from the protest against the authority of the Church at the Reformation. Since the authority of the Church was denied, some other authority had to be accepted. The parallel authority of Holy Scripture was put forward. Then came the obvious difficulty, that, since there was no external authoritative Church, there was no one to tell you what Holy Scripture meant, and you were thrown back on the interpretation which each individual might make of any passage in the Bible, or its general sense. For instance (to take the leading example) the individual had to decide for himself what was meant by the words of Consecration. But the modern extension of the thing has gone far beyond such comparatively orthodox limits as trusting to the authority of Holy Scripture, even under private interpretation. It has taken the form of basing religion upon individual feelings. Men and women say: "This is true, because it is true to me. I have felt this, and therefore I know it to be true."

Of these subjective sects the most curious, though not the most powerful at the present moment, is the strange system called Christian Science. No doubt tomorrow another will succeed it, and after that yet another; but today it is Christian Science which stands out most prominently as the type of a subjective sect. Its votaries, of course, will tell us of much that it includes besides its most striking tenet; but that most striking tenet is sufficient to characterize it. The faithful of the sect are asked to regard the individual mental attitude towards evil, and especially physical evil, as a purely subjective phenomenon. Persuade yourself that it is not there, and it is not there. Hence powers of healing and all the rest of it.

Now these counter-religions, opponents to and, in their little way, rivals of the Catholic Church, have two characteristics apparently contradictory but not really so. One is the permanence of the phenomenon, the other is the ephemeral quality of individual instances. They are always cropping up—especially today—but they are also perpetually disappearing after a short life.

I would like to concentrate upon the second characteristic, to show why I do not regard any one of these counter-religions of the subjective sort as a serious menace to Catholicism.

The sectarian of these vagaries is often intense and always sincere. Based as her (sometimes his) mood is upon personal enthusiasm and personal spiritual experiences, it brooks no contradiction. But it does not last, because it makes no appeal to that fundamental necessity of the human reason for external proof. I may be told that it does so in the particular case of Christian Science which appeals to actual cures. But there is not sufficient volume and persistence of such cures. Moreover, the claim made is at issue with the common sense of mankind.

It is here that the various forms of subjective religion show themselves so much weaker than Spiritualism; for Spiritualism, as we shall see, bases itself on controllable positive proof. Amid a mass of fraud there is a certain residue of ascertainable evidence; and though much of that evidence may be shaken there is a remainder which cannot be denied. Spiritualism appeals to something which the human race has always demanded, to wit, external evidence verifiable by a number of independent means. Your purely subjective religion does not appeal to such evidence. It appeals to intensity of enthusiasm, and to little more. Hence its lack of substance, its probable lack of endurance.

Here it may be objected: "If you say that this or that sect, based on such mere emotions and wholly subjective in character, cannot form the seed of an organized Universal Religion; what about the Catholic Church, which Herself arose from such a beginning of enthusiasm and illusion?"

The parallel is wholly false.

Nothing is commoner than for those who are ill-acquainted with the early history of the Catholic Church and of the society in which it arose, to explain the origin of Catholicism in these terms. They put it forward as a subjective religion, confirmed by some marvelous cures which were real and a host of imaginary events which men only accepted because they were in an abnormal state of mind.

But has Catholicism really been like this in its origins it would never have survived. It survived because it appealed also to the general sense of mankind; because it fitted in with what mankind knew of itself and its needs, and of what it lacked to satisfy such needs; also because it confirmed itself every day in the lives of those subjected to it; because, of the wonders put forward, the greatest of all—the Resurrection—was reluctantly witnessed to by opponents; but most of all *because it maintained unity.* The Catholic Church was from Her origin a thing, not a theory. She was a society informing the individual, and not a mass of individuals forming a society. From Her very beginning She tracked down heresy and expelled it. She is a kingdom. Subjective religion is a private whim. Though it must continue an unceasing form of error so long as men refuse authority and are strongly subject to religious emotion, it will never build up a rival church. As a general tendency, especially while it still inherits the general ethic of its Protestant origins three hundred years old, it is an influence hostile to Catholicism; but its various products have not the stuff of permanence in them. They have not in them a sufficient correspondence with reality to create any one formidable opponent. Spiritualism has such correspondence with real (objective) phenomena.

What of Spiritualism?

When I examine Spiritualism from the outside I notice certain characteristics about it which are very remarkable.

In the first place there is a positiveness, an unquestioning and sober conviction which is quite different from the hysteria of the sects and which it is of the highest interest to note and analyze.

This conviction is not of the nature of Faith, properly so-called. Faith is a virtue, a grace, and an act of the *will*. The essential of Faith is an *acceptation,* upon authority, of things unseen; that is a refusal by the *will* to admit the opposite of a proposition, although experimental proof be lacking. But Spiritualism holds its convictions upon sensible, or supposedly sensible, experience; that is, upon experimental proof.

Now that is a new note altogether in the story of modern religions. The Presbyterian, the Lutheran, the Baptist and the rest did not say that they held their tenets through a direct personal experience of the senses. Neither Zwingle nor any other Heresiarch claimed that they had seen or heard the things which they believed. On the contrary, apart from their novel doctrines they retained a great mass of the ancient Catholic dogmas such as the Incarnation, the Trinity, etc., which of their essence are transcendental, and cannot be witnessed to by the senses. But Spiritualism says: "I have physical evidence of those things hitherto called supernatural, and it is upon that physical evidence I base myself, not upon an internal emotion or 'religious experience' as does the typical Protestant sectarian today, nor on Authority as does every Catholic."

I think we ought to recognize how strong a foundation is this appeal to positive evidence, and what a fixed type of certitude it produces. I could quote the case of a man for whom I have the highest respect; one of the best living writers of the English language, who was frankly and openly an atheist and materialist till he was quite elderly, and who, being a very sincere man, made no concealment of his philosophy. He denied the survival of the soul and even the existence of God. This man by his own testimony (and he would be the last person to affirm anything he believed to be false) heard at a séance the voice—and, if I remember rightly, saw the face as well—of someone he had deeply loved and who was dead. He bore witness to this sight and hearing to myself and to the world. This man I have personally known and shall always revere.

Note further that all those who support Spiritualism talk in the same fashion. We have a prominent popular writer of fiction, a great physicist, and many other names drawn from every kind of intellectual pursuit repeating with passionate earnestness that "the thing is proved," that those who deny it are willfully refusing to examine plain testimony, and that anyone who will impartially do so will be convinced.

Now it may be contended that none of the phenomena, for which there is indeed a great body of testimony, have necessarily the character claimed for them. Many (for instance, the mentioning by a medium of things only known to one of those present) may be explained by what is a certainly proved fact and established (though abnormal and seemingly not of this world)—telepathy. Others (for instance, the seeing of a face or the hearing of a voice) may be set down to illusion. But it seems to be the general agreement of those who have gone deeply into the matter—and not less of those who abhor Spiritualism than of those who revere it—that there is, when all is explained (trickery, illusion and the rest of it) a certain balance of what we should call transcendental experience. You may meet many a man and woman in the case of the one I quoted; people who have become convinced of what are called "the truth of Spiritualism" after having been, like most of us, contemptuously skeptical. But the other process, the man who has believed in it and lost faith, is perhaps unknown, or at any rate very rare. Here then I say is the first mark of the thing, the strength of its conviction.

There is a great deal of tomfoolery about it (the spirits of the dead drinking whisky and smoking cigars: talking base journalese: playing silly little tricks and practical jokes). But when all this is allowed for, some real experience does remain, and on that real experience is based the intense conviction of which I have spoken.

Now there is a second mark in connection with spiritualism which renders it a considerable opponent, and it is a mark not usually recognized: its venerable lineage.

The thing, though of today in its existing form, is in essence as old as human record. It is one with witchcraft, necromancy, magic. What seems novel in it to us, only so seems novel because it has come after a period of rationalism. The average educated man of the nineteenth century thought that all the talk of all the centuries about witchcraft and demonology and the rest was too absurd to be worth noticing. He laughed it out of court. But his view was not a sound one historically. Whether such phenomena have occurred in the past is a matter to debate upon the evidence, but that mankind in the overwhelming mass of its extension in time and in space, that is, over much the greater part of the world and over much the greater part of its recorded history, *has* believed that such things go on, cannot be denied.

The fact that this very new religion is also nothing but a resurrection of a very old one, adds to its strength and to the seriousness with which we must regard it.

Catholic doctrine upon the matter is well-known. All such investigation is forbidden as an immortal act. It is either playing with falsehood, or (if there be, or where there be reality in it) it is of evil origin. We do not communicate with the blessed dead save in those very rare experiences which God may grant to a very few as visions. If we communicate with spirits of another world at will, summoning them regularly for our purposes, the spirits with which we are dealing are evil spirits. That is the teaching of the Church on this matter from the beginning to this our day.

We know (it may be said in passing) that its votaries are sometimes driven mad, sometimes exhibit all the phenomena of Possession, and that even its strictest supporters admit these practices to be perilous and only to be engaged in cautiously.

Everyone who has read that striking book by the late Father Hugh Benson, *The Necromancers,* will remember the true drawing of the sincere medium and that medium's admission of the peril which his creed and practice involved.

There, then, are the two main features so far as I can analyze them of this strange new sect: (1) The quality of its certitude based, not upon emotion, but upon experiment: (2) The very deep roots in the human past from which it springs; the antiquity of the doctrine and practice of which it is but the resurrection.

Yet it has not in it the seed of a great new religion, and the reason should be plain. It enjoys advantages common to all research: it has experiment and evidence to work on. But it suffers the corresponding disadvantages. It has nothing of revelation in it, no unity of Philosophy, no general reply to the great questions and therefore no Authority. It takes on no body: it has no organization. That it will persist I believe. That it will grow is probable. That it will become a Church is not possible, for it is not made of the stuff of Universality out of which great organisms arise.

Where then shall we look for the seed of a New Religion? I should reply, tentatively, in this: the satisfaction of that Messianic mood with which, paradoxically, the despair of the New Paganism is shot. The expectation of better things—the confident expectation of their advent—affects the vileness and folly of our time everywhere. Let an individual appear with the capacity or chance to crystallize these hopes and the enemy will have arrived. For anti-Christ will be a man.

# 6

## THE OPPORTUNITY

The New Paganism advances over the modern world like a blight over a harvest. You may see it in building, in drawing, in letters, in morals.

But it seems—as yet—to be producing no positive force. It is breeding no new organized religion to combat the Faith. That may come. Meanwhile there is a gap: and that gap is our Opportunity. It is possible to reconvert the world.

What weapons can Catholicism discover wherewith to reconquer from Paganism the advance which it shall have made in our culture?

This Opportunity presented to Catholicism has two aspects. The first is, that Paganism being of its nature a confessed inability to answer the Great Questions on Man's nature and destiny, is of its nature an invitation to those who possess the key. The second is that we are dealing, not with a Paganism native to those we have to meet, but with a Paganism which is a corruption of, and decline from, a much better state of society, some memory of which remains, and the corruption of which may soon prove sufficiently shocking to provoke reaction. We are still dealing with Christendom: with Christendom in ruins, but with Christendom. Our fathers aid us.

As to the first, our unique power to answer the Great Questions, it has always seemed to me the most powerful instrument possessed by the Faith in the spiritual crisis now so close upon us. You cannot perhaps convert despair when despair has been erected into a system, as it has in the greater part of Asiatic Paganism; but you can check it in its beginnings, when it is no more than the loss of something which the despairing man knows he has enjoyed, and cannot but wish he might recover. To the Great Questions which man must ask himself and which so insistently demand an answer (What is man? Whence comes he? Has the universe a purpose? What part does man play in that purpose? What final destinies may be his?) the Catholic Church gives not only a reply (Buddhism does that after a fashion, and even in a very vague manner other Paganisms less systematized) but a fully consistent solution: a sound, complete, system of philosophy. Moreover Her answer is not only consistent; it is triumphant. She knows fully her own validity; She can point in actual practice to the effect of happiness produced in society by Her philosophy.

Those Great Questions will be asked again and again. We are not hearing the last of them; we are rather at the beginnings of their second postulation, at the beginnings of a new interest in them.

It is a strange mark of the New Paganism, and the most hopeful one, that it should already have become occupied, with *discussion* at least, on the problem of Man. But the greater part of our Neo-Pagans remain throughout the discussion in ignorance of what the Catholic scheme may be. The success or failure of our effort against the New Paganism will depend much more on letting people know what the Catholic Church *is,* than upon anything else.

It is arresting to discover in what numbers modern men with a reasonable standard of instruction in the rest of the world about them are blank upon the most important subject of all; though it lies everywhere right to their hand. They have not the A.B.C. of the Faith.

Here in England, where I am writing these lines, not a day passes but someone, often of eminence, starts a theological controversy in the popular Press, makes an affirmation, one way or the other, upon the Great Questions, and proposes an answer. But in the whole mass of the stuff—and there are thousands of columns of it—there is not one hundredth which shows the least acquaintance with what the Catholic Church may be: the

Catholic theology and its two thousand years of accumulated definition and reason: the philosophy which made our civilization and in the absence of which our civilization may perish.

Thus an Anglican Bishop, Dr. Barnes of Birmingham, a man distinguished in his University, a very clear writer and, one would have said, compelled by his very profession to read some theology, told us his reasons the other day for denying the Catholic doctrine of the Resurrection. He said it was incompatible with *chemistry!* Evidently he had no idea what the Catholic doctrine might be.

Sir Oliver Lodge, a physicist, produced somewhat earlier a strong affirmation of the future life. It turned out to be this life: much as it is lived in the clubs and hotels of his acquaintance. He has never heard, apparently, the Catholic doctrine of Eternity, nor the implications of that doctrine, nor so much as an echo of the profound speculations, the profounder conclusions, which contemplation of Catholic dogma has reached in that awful affair.

These are two typical examples from England. Of course, things are better on the continent of Europe where there is some acquaintance with scholastic philosophy even among the opponents of the Catholic Church. But everywhere the chief need is *instruction,* and our greatest weakness in the conflict which has begun is the difficulty of getting our opponents to know the mere nature of the subject they are so ready to discuss.

The second opportunity we have is of a different sort, not intellectual but moral. The falling of Christendom into Paganism must necessarily produce results shocking to our inherited culture.

Of this reaction there are already signs, but how far will it be pushed? Left to itself that reaction will effect little. The more hopeful Catholic is encouraged when he sees the disgust already provoked by the first products of the new Paganism. He notes the appeal still presented by traditional morals, by the desire to save beauty and proportion and decent living. The less hopeful Catholic notes the vast and increasing proportion of the world about him in which such disgust is not aroused: on which the worst innovations meet with no protest, though commonly, it is true, with no welcome. He sees the continued progress of slime and the gradual (or rapid) swamping of province after province in our ancient culture.

How far the reaction may go, whether we may not even be able to lead it to a triumphant conclusion, no man can tell. I cannot but wish—somewhat temerariously—that the new Paganism may develop a little too rapidly, shock a little too violently the dormant conscience of Europe, and thereby prepare the counter-attack against it.

\* \* \*

Our world finds itself moving towards nothingness; can it remain content in the prospect of such a goal?

All the old goals have disappeared. Civil liberty has not done what was asked of it, it has not even been achieved. Its concomitant, so-called "democracy," has not done what was asked of it, it has not given man dignity or security. Both these great ideals of the 19th century are ending in mere plutocracy and in our subjection to a few quite unworthy controllers of all our lives: the monopolists of material, of currency, information and transport; the tyranny of trust-masters in production, banking, journals and communications.

The lay philosophies have gone. They have all broken down. They are no longer in effect. They fulfilled no ultimate function; they solved no problem, they brought no peace. Their power has departed.

Even the noble religion of Nationalism has only brought us to the mutual self-destruction of the Great War and threat of much worse: and Nationalism itself is growing weary. It made its supreme effort in compelling men to muster for the huge slaughter; it will hardly so muster them again.

The void which I thus indicate is not only negative. It creates what engineers call "a potential," just as a void in nature creates a "a potential." For a void must be filled. Therefore the emptiness of the present moment, and its unrest, have a certain most important, positive effect; and that is the Opportunity. We live not only in a moment of confusion, disappointment and anger, but also in a moment of Opportunity for the Faith.

I have discussed in the last section what signs there might be of new Counter-Religions arising against the Faith and said that, as yet, none appeared. I said also that though not *certain* yet such a creation was *probable.* I add here that in its delay is the Opportunity for the Faith to take the initiative again after its long siege of 300 years.

Some solution, as we saw in the discussion of New Arrivals, will presumably be attempted; some creed, some social philosophy in which men can rest. Nor will the process perhaps be very long delayed. Mankind of our sort seems unlikely to carry on for long without certitude, real or imaginary. Our minds need something on which to bite and should sooner or later, and sooner rather than later, erect doctrines of which tradition will make an unshaken system; men should adopt not only conventions of conduct, but a code of morals; they should discover or invent something to worship. We of the Faith can present them something real to discover, which, when they have found it, will destroy any desire to invent.

Such is the nature of the Opportunity—and it is of deep interest. Perhaps there has never been an occasion in history when interest of the same kind was present in the same degree.

\* \* \*

Perhaps it is more than an Opportunity. Perhaps action has already begun.

The men of a particular period are not aware of the forces that arise in their day. Men in the mass appreciate a force when it is mature and when its action has begun to produce effects upon a large scale. When it is nascent its presence goes either unnoticed or despised.

There is present today throughout the civilization of Europe and its expansion over the New World, a force of this kind; it is the recovery of the Catholic Apologetic.

It is curious to note that the power of this new influence is more readily recognized by the opponents of the Catholic

Church than by its friends. These last are too much aware of the old anti-Catholic fashion in history and literature. They exaggerate its survival and are timid.

On the top of that there is the desire not to disturb. What is worse, the very philosophy of our opponents has tinctured our supporters. Among the less-cultivated the connection between religion and its secondary social effects is unfamiliar. Among the somewhat more cultivated there is the fear of disturbing superficial worldly relations. Even in the highest rank of intelligence and sincerity there has grown up a sort of habit in accepting insult, and a *vis inertiae* which inhibits the Catholic from doing freely what his opponents do freely. Yet the Catholic apologetic grows.

This new force, the modern Catholic apologetic, is fought shy of, even by those in whose favor it is working; but to convince yourself of its existence, note two things: the rapidity with which its opponents have discovered its presence, and the change in general tone now running like a tide through the thought of our time.

A new antagonism to the new force of the Catholic Church shows itself in nations of Protestant culture by a certain note of exasperation which in the day of our fathers was unknown. There was plenty of active opposition and bludgeoning of the Church in mid-Victorian days; but it was a contemptuous and assured anger: that of today is panicky. In nations of the Catholic culture the ill-at-ease Catholic advance shows itself in a sort of sullen muttering among our opponents; the complaint of an old cause which thinks its success a matter of right but no longer certain.

If we turn to the positive evidences of this Catholic advance we shall discover these only after a very general fashion.

The characteristically modern test of numbers fails. We are not as yet rapidly advancing in numbers. But the numerical test does not apply at first to a rising moral force. A modern man accustomed to testing everything by numbers, would, if he had been put down in Rome about the year 280, have decided that the Catholic Church had no chance—but he would have been quite wrong.

In numbers, I repeat, the Catholic Church is not advancing appreciably in the modern world. I think that on the whole, in mere numbers, She is slightly receding. Great peasant areas in France have been lost, and in all Catholic countries great numbers of the new working-class suburbs of the towns have been lost: and these losses more than compensate, on a mere counting of heads, for the new recruitment among the thinkers.

In Ireland there may now be some increase over twenty years ago, especially since the stoppage of emigration after 1914. I have no statistics by me as I write; but certainly, compared with a lifetime ago, the figures are against the Faith even there. Whether they be so in Great Britain or no I cannot tell—nor can anyone else—for there is no satisfactory record; but I doubt whether the increase through conversion and the bringing up of the children of mixed marriages has either compensated for the leakage or proved equivalent to the general increase of the population.

Here I am subject to correction by many good observers who will disagree with me. But, at any rate, their margin of disagreement will not be very wide. In Italy and Spain, where the position has been firm now for many years, there have been lost throughout two generations, and especially latterly, great bodies of artisans in the new industrialism. The bulk of the Germans have been subjected for a long lifetime to an anti-Catholic hegemony; in certain Slav States, notably in Bohemia, Nationalism lost, or weakened, Catholic numbers.

But the more important intellectual and moral tests of the advance are all in our favor. To begin with, the Catholic case has "got over the footlights." It has "pierced." Intellectual Europe today is again aware of the one consistent philosophy upon this earth which explains our little passage through the daylight; which gives a purpose to things and which presents not a mere hodgepodge of stories and unfounded assertions, but a whole chain and body of cause and effect in the moral world. It is further becoming apparent that there is, as yet, no rival in this respect to the Catholic Church. There is now no full alternative system left.

Of perhaps more effect in a time such as ours, after so long a prevalence of intellectual decline, is the pragmatic test of the Faith, that is, its test in practice; for practice and experience affect even those who cannot think.

It has become more and more clear in the last generation, and with particular acceleration since the latest and immense catastrophe of the Great War, that the Faith preserves whatever, outside the Faith, is crumbling: marriage, the family, property, authority, honor to parents, right reason, even the arts. This is a political fact—not a theory. It is a fact as large and as certain as is a neighboring mountain in a landscape.

If the influence of the Church declines, civilization will decline with it and all the effects of tradition. It is a commonplace with educated men that the Catholic Church made our civilization, but it is not equally a commonplace—as it ought to be—that on Her continued power depends the continuance of our civilization. Our civilization is as much a product of the Catholic Church as the vine is the product of a particular climate. Take the vine to another climate and it will die.

It is error to mistake this product of the Catholic Church, Civilization, for her true end and nature. Her nature is that of an infallible and divine voice. Her end is beatitude elsewhere for us all: who here are exiles. But my point is that all men should closely watch the fortunes of the Faith, both those who accept it and those who reject it, because that fortune is bound up with all those lesser things which even those who reject the Church regard as essential to right living, from the lesser arts and amenities to the main institutions of European society.

Those who defend and support the Church (though believing it to be but a man-made illusion) because it happens to be the support of a temporal structure, are in grave moral and theological error. The Faith is not to be supported on such grounds. My thesis is not of that kind—God forbid!—but rather that all men believing or unbelieving should fix their close attention, at this moment of revolution and transition, upon the Catholic Church, as being the pivotal institution whereupon the fate, even temporal, of all must turn.

Two things still partly mask that truth: chaotic and feverish industralism and the idea that tradition can be destroyed and yet life remain. For the second I would say that those who maintain it do not understand the nature of life, of maturity, of a fixed organism—from which if you take away its vital principle the whole decays. While as to the first, industrialism, I should say that it has lived its odd diseased life (strangely and suddenly expanding, but without sufficient happiness) by what it retains of Catholic doctrine. Insofar as Industrialism and its bad commercial morals have lived with any health—and health is not their conspicuous feature—that non-Catholic culture has hitherto lived by retaining some sense of moral responsibility, and I might add (however distantly) of the Incarnation—of the Incarnation's effect, at least, upon human dignity. It has survived on ideas inherited from a better time. Moreover today the non-Catholic culture is manifestly failing, and its only issue is towards nothingness—even more among its Pagan rich than among its now rebellious poor.

*　*　*

I apprehend that in the near future there will arise grave difficulties from the very fact that the tide of the Faith is rising. Those engaged upon helping on that tide will confuse Faith with fads. For this peril a recognition of authority is the first and indeed the only safeguard. Moreover, *we* have no doubt where Authority lies, and therein we are singularly fortunate, for we act under obedience to a Society of Divine Foundation, of known and definable organs for its expression, and of infallibility in its final decisions.

And upon the right conduct of our passage through such perils, how much depends! Upon the right conduct of the presentation of the Faith in the next long lifetime surely depends the future of the world.

There would seem to be no third event between two issues. Either we shall see the gradual permeation of mankind by the only body of truth to which the mind leaps in unison, rendering all as secure as it can be among a fallen race; or our civilization will sink to be a completely alien body, knowing even less of the Faith than do the distraught town millions of today.

It would seem as though, before the youngest of our children has passed, the world will have had to take its decision between these two alternatives: either the spreading of the Faith throughout the now closely intercommunicating body of mankind, or the splitting of that vast association into two camps: one small, and perhaps dwindling, of the fold; the other large, perhaps growing larger, upon the hills without.

Not a few profound observers (one in especial, a modern French-Jewish convert of the highest intellectual power) have proposed, as a probable tendency or goal to which we were moving, a world in which a small but intense body of the Faith should stand apart in an increasing flood of Paganism. I, for my part (it is but a personal opinion and worth little) believe, upon the whole, a Catholic increase to be the more likely; for, in spite of the time in which I live, I cannot believe that the Human Reason will permanently lose its power. Now the Faith is based upon Reason, and everywhere outside the Faith the decline of Reason is apparent.

But if I be asked what sign we may look for to show that the advance of the Faith is at hand, I would answer by a word the modern world has forgotten: Persecution. When that shall once more be at work it will be morning.

# ABOUT THE AUTHOR

**Hilaire Belloc**
**1870-1953**

The great Hilaire Belloc was likely the most famous and influential Catholic historian of the past two centuries. His rare understanding of the central role of the Catholic Faith in forming Western Civilization—from the time of Christ up to our own—still opens the eyes of many today.

Hilaire Belloc was born in 1870 at La Celle, St. Cloud, France. His father was a distinguished French lawyer; his mother was English. After his father's death, the family moved to England. Hilaire did his military service in France, then returned to Balliol College, Oxford, taking first-class honors in history when he graduated in 1895. It has been said that his ambition was to rewrite the Catholic history of his two fatherlands, France and England. In 1896 he married Elodie Hogan of Napa, California; the marriage was blessed with two sons and two daughters.

During a period of 50 years—until he suffered a stroke in 1946—Hilaire Belloc wrote over a hundred books on history, economics, military science and travel, plus novels and poetry. He also wrote hundreds of magazine and newspaper articles. He served for a time as a member of the English House of Commons and edited a paper called the *Eye-Witness.*

As an historian, Belloc is largely responsible for correcting the once nearly universal *Whig* interpretation of British history, which attributed Britain's greatness to her Anglo-Saxon and Protestant background.

Hilaire Belloc visited the United States several times, giving guest lectures at both Notre Dame and Fordham Universities. Among his most famous books are *The Great Heresies, Survivals and New Arrivals* (something of a sequel to the above), *The Path to Rome, Characters of the Reformation,* and *How the Reformation Happened.* Hilaire Belloc died in 1953, leaving behind a great legacy of insight regarding the true, though largely unrecognized, inspirer of Western Civilization—the Catholic Church.